FREE
TO BE
ME

Tim Hawkins

FREE TO BE ME

How the death of Jesus changes everything

10 Publishing

a division of 10 ofthose.com

Unless otherwise stated, Scripture quotations are taken from THE HOLY BIBLE, NEW INTERNATIONAL VERSION (Anglicised Edition). Copyright © 1979, 1984, 2011 by Biblica (formerly International Bible Society). Used by permission of Hodder & Stoughton Publishers. All rights reserved. 'NIV' is a registered trademark of Biblica. UK trademark number 1448790.

Copyright © 2020 by Tim Hawkins

First published in Great Britain in 2020

The right of Tim Hawkins to be identified as the Author of this Work has been asserted by him in accordance with the Copyright, Designs and Patents Act 1988.

All rights reserved. No part of this publication may be reproduced, stored in a retrieval system or transmitted in any form or by any means, electronic, mechanical, photocopying, recording or otherwise, without the prior permission of the publisher or the Copyright Licensing Agency.

British Library Cataloguing in Publication Data
A record for this book is available from the British Library

ISBN: 978-1-912373-94-9

Designed by Jude May
Cover image © Slavaleks | iStock
Internal image © MicrovOne | iStock

Printed in Denmark by Nørhaven

10Publishing, a division of 10ofthose.com
Unit C, Tomlinson Road, Leyland, PR25 2DY, England
Email: info@10ofthose.com
Website: www.10ofthose.com

1 3 5 7 10 8 6 4 2

CONTENTS

Section 5. Free To Obey

Section 6. The Last Bit

SECTION 1

Created To Be Free

I Want To Be Free

Wouldn't it be brilliant to be free? To have nobody else telling you what to do. Imagine what it would be like if you didn't have to keep the rules that somebody else had made up for you. You could do your own thing. Be your own person. Dream your own dreams.

That's what I wanted when I was at school. Everybody else had their own expectations as to what I should be like. My parents wanted me to be successful. My teachers wanted me to work hard. My friends wanted me to be the same as they were. They didn't like people who were different. But there was something within me that just wanted to do things my own way.

When I started school as a little 5-year-old boy, nobody wanted any of us to stand out as individuals. They dressed us all in the same school uniforms so we all looked identical.

We sat in rows of desks and all did the same lessons. The boys played boy-games and the girls played girl-games. And if I didn't want to be laughed at by all my friends, I quickly learned that I wasn't meant to hang out with the girls. They picked on me and said I'd get 'girl-germs'. But there was a particular girl that I liked. And I thought it would be really cool to be the first boy at school to have a girlfriend. But I had a problem. Not only was it not 'cool' for a boy to hang out with the girls, but how on earth would I ever let her know that I liked her? Life, girls and relationships can be tough for a 5-year-old boy.

So, I devised a cunning plan. I worked out how I would let her know that I liked her. I decided that … *I would sit down in her lap.* Okay – looking back now, it was probably a silly idea, but as a 5-year-old boy – I thought it would work.

I planned my moment. It was lunchtime, and everybody was sitting down outside having their lunch. I saw the girl of my dreams eating there. I carefully manoeuvred into position. Now was my moment … I got close to her and I made my move. In an attempt to claim the crown for being the first boy in school to get a girlfriend, I walked straight in front of her – and sat down in her lap! I had struck a blow for individuality! I was finally doing my own thing!

The one thing I didn't realise was that for lunch that day she was eating a meat pie. She had the meat pie precariously balanced on her lap. When I sat down in her lap, I sat square in the middle of her meat pie! When I stood up, I had huge chunks of gravy, meat and pastry all over my little blue shorts. All the other kids laughed at me and called me 'pie-pants'. I was ridiculed by the boys; laughed at by the girls; and reprimanded by my teachers. It's a tough life for a 5-year-old boy who wants to be an individual.

You might not have done anything as silly as I did, but I'm sure you have felt the frustration of simply wanting to escape from everybody else's expectations. Everybody else wants you to fit in with their plan. There are rules to be obeyed; expectations to be fulfilled; regulations to conform to … It seems like everybody else has a plan for what sort of person you're going to be. And I'm sure at some stage you have wanted to run away from it all and just yell out 'I want to be me!'

Have You Ever Wanted To Run Away?
You might be dealing with some serious stuff. There could be huge hassles with your boyfriend or girlfriend. Maybe everything is a bit tense at home and you're looking for any opportunity to hang out somewhere else. Perhaps you and your mum had a shouting match this morning. Maybe things aren't going well between your mum and your dad and you're not even sure they're both going to be there for you when you get home. Maybe your grades aren't great at school. Maybe *life* isn't great at school. Maybe there's something from which you're struggling to break free.

Teenagers have to deal with so much pressure these days. There's a whole variety of people who will tell you that you're not good enough. There's an endless supply of critics who will point out your every mistake. Our culture teaches us that to survive we should call out everyone else's mistakes and weaknesses. But you know how awful it feels when everyone is pointing out your mistakes.

Sometimes you just want to be free. You want to be free to be the person that you really want to be. You want to be free to be the person that *God* really wants you to be. You just want to be you. But you can't do it. Everywhere you turn there's someone else who wants to control your life. Every time you try to get up there's someone who wants to push you back down. You just want to be you, but *everyone* else wants you to be *someone* else. There are always rules you have to follow. Someone else has got a better plan than you have.

Sometimes it can feel like God is one of those people who gets in the way. You want to be the real you, but you can't. You have to be the 'Christian' you. Everyone else gets to do what they feel like – but you – you have to obey what God says – you have to ask the question 'What Would Jesus Do?' I'm sure there's been a moment where you've felt like breaking free from God. Maybe you've seen some of your friends give up and walk away from Jesus. Perhaps you've reached the point of wanting to give up as well. Maybe reading this book is your last-ditch attempt to hang in there with Jesus for just one more day.

I don't know why you're reading this book. Maybe it was a present from a helpful relative? Perhaps the title intrigued you? Maybe you're just plain bored? I don't know why you're here. But I believe it is no accident that you are here. God has brought you here because he wants to challenge you and change your heart. He wants to release you from whatever is holding you back in your life. He wants you to be liberated to become the person that he has destined you to be.

God doesn't want you held captive by other people's criticisms. He doesn't want you dragged back by your failures and mistakes. He doesn't want you weighed down by your own sin that you find so hard to deal with. God wants you to break free from all that. God wants you to be released to achieve the destiny that he has created for you. God wants you to experience the joy of being free to be his precious child. Are you ready to meet God in his Word? Are you ready to be *truly free?*

God Made Me To Be Free

Did you know that when God designed you, he planned for you to be free? Did you know that when God created you, he formed you to perfection and gave you *an inbuilt freedom?* Let's look in the Bible to see the magnificent person that God has designed you to be.

God Made Me In His Image

> *Then God said, 'Let us make mankind in our image, in our likeness …'*
> *So God created mankind in his own image,*
> *in the image of God he created them;*
> *male and female he created them (Genesis 1:26–27).*

Do you see what God is saying about you? You have been hand-crafted by a master designer – you are created *in God's image*. This sounds good. But what does it mean to be an *image* of something?

Being made in God's image doesn't mean that God has created you to *look* like he does. But it means God has made you to *be* like he is. You're meant to have the same sort of characteristics that God has:

- God is loving, so you are designed to be loving
- God is forgiving, so you are designed to be forgiving
- God hates sin, so you are designed to hate sin
- God is generous, so you are designed to be generous

It's almost as if God said: 'I am going to make some creatures who will be able to show everyone what I am like. When people look at these human beings, they'll get a picture of the sort of God that I am.' That's who you are. You were created in God's image. It means that when people see you, they get an idea of what God is like. *God created you so that when people see you, they get an idea of what God is really like.* Wow! You get to show other people the wonders of our magnificent God! Let me show you one of the main ways that God says you are just like him.

God Made Me To Rule His World

> *Then God said, 'Let us make mankind in our image, in our likeness, so that they may rule over the fish in the sea and the birds in the sky, over the livestock and all the wild animals, and over all the creatures that move along the ground' (Genesis 1:26).*

If God says that the reason he made you was so that you would be able to show the world what he is like, then the main way you are to show what God is like is by ruling over all the rest the world. God wants you to help run his world the same way that *he* would run it. God has given you the freedom to be a world ruler but only because of who he made you to be. He has made you *in his image.* You have the freedom to run this world – while you do it the way God does. You are free to be the person that God has designed you to be – provided that you stay dependent on him. Your freedom to be truly you is absolutely tied up with you remaining reliant on God. If you throw away being dependent on him – you throw away your freedom.

It's like walking in front of the mirror. What you see in the mirror is an image of yourself. If you throw away the mirror, the image is no longer there. In the same way, you are made in the image of God. You reflect what God is like. But if you say: 'I don't want to do things God's way, I don't want God in the picture' and move your mirror away from

God, then his image can no longer be seen in you. You are only free to be the person that God has designed you to be when you keep reflecting his image by being totally dependent on him.

'What do you mean? To be free I have to depend on God? I thought the whole idea of being free was that I didn't have to depend on anyone?'

Let's just backtrack for a moment and look at what freedom really is. You have been created with an *inbuilt dependency* on God. If you stop depending on him, then *you lose your freedom*. It's like a train – a locomotive engine. Trains are designed to have an inbuilt dependency on the rails. They're made that way! While the train stays dependant on the rails, it is free to be a train.

Let's imagine that the train has been around for a few years. It's sort of going through puberty, it's getting sick of being told what to do and it just wants to do its own thing.

Why do I have to go where those stupid rails tell me to go? I wanna go where I wanna go! I wanna be free!

The train decides to do its own thing. It goes off the rails. It wants to go to the shops. It wants to go through the McDonald's Drive-Thru. It wants to go and play on the beach. Just imagine for a moment that a train could do that. If a train could go off the rails and just meander wherever it felt like, what do you think would happen to that train? It's going to grind to a halt quick smart! It's going to smash into things. It's going to get bogged down. If that train goes off the rails and does its own thing, then it's going nowhere.

As soon as it goes off the rails – it grinds to a halt. As soon as it goes off the rails – it loses its freedom to be a train. All because it was designed with an inbuilt dependency on those rails.

In the same way, you have been designed with an inbuilt dependency on God. Sometimes you can think that being free is going *off the rails* with God and just doing whatever you feel like. But as soon as you give up depending on God for your every breath, as soon as you give up depending on God for your every step:

- you lose your freedom to be truly human
- you get bogged down in your own sin
- you smash into relationships and destroy them

You have been designed with an inbuilt dependency on God. When you give up depending on him – *you lose your freedom*. God gave you that freedom. He has made you as a world ruler. And he makes everything in the world for you to enjoy. Not only has God designed you to be *free*, he has also designed you to be *the best!*

God Made Me To Be The Best

Who Am I?

That is the question that bugs the whole of humanity.

> *'Who am I really?'*
> *'Tell me what my purpose is!'*
> *'I want to get in touch with the real me!'*
> *'The entire cosmos is so big, where do I fit in?'*

The Bible asks that question – and the Bible answers it. Have you ever noticed that when you read the Bible, you find that one part of the Bible explains another part? We're going to check out Psalm 8. The writer of this psalm has obviously been reading Genesis 1, and it leads him to ask an obvious question:

> *When I consider your heavens,*
> *the work of your fingers,*
> *the moon and the stars,*
> *which you have set in place,*
> *what is mankind that you are mindful of them,*
> *human beings that you care for them? (Psalm 8:3–4).*

When we look at the whole universe – and we see how big it is, how spectacular it is, how powerful, how complex, how enormous – it can make us question our place in creation. Who are we? What is it about us that would cause God to care for us? Now – what answer are you expecting? If you didn't know what line comes next in Psalm 8, what would be the normal answer to this question?

> *'Compared to the whole universe – I'm nothing.'*
> *'An insignificant speck!'*
> *'There's God – then there's the angels and the heavenly beings – then there's the galaxies, and the solar systems, and the whole of life as we know it – then there's me.'*
> *'Insignificant.'*
> *'Compared to the whole of the cosmos – I'm nothing.'*

Do you ever feel like compared with the wonders of creation, compared with the annals of cosmic history, compared with the accomplishments of myriads of civilisations that, basically, you don't stack up too well? If we read on in Psalm 8, God tells us exactly where we fit into the whole of his cosmos.

God Crowns Me With Honour

> *When I consider your heavens,*
> *the work of your fingers,*
> *the moon and the stars,*
> *which you have set in place,*
> *what is mankind that you are mindful of them,*
> *. human beings that you care for them? (Psalm 8:3–4).*

Here's the answer in the next verse!

> *You have made them a little lower than the angels and crowned them with glory and honour (Psalm 8:5).*

Have you got it? In the scope of the entire cosmos:

- first there's God ...
- then there are the angels ...
- then there's *you* ...
- and then there's everything else!

God has made *you* just a little lower than the angels, and has crowned *you* with glory and honour! We often talk about how important it is that we give glory and honour to God. And yes – that is important. But this verse is talking about *how God gives glory and honour to you.* When God designed you, he created you to be a person who is worthy of great glory and great honour.

One more time … just so you get it straight:

- first there's God …
- then there are the angels …
- then there's *you* …
- and then there's everything else!

Just let that soak in for a moment. Rather than putting you near the bottom of his food chain, God has given you one of the highest places in his universe. He has placed you just below the angels. Is that how you think of yourself? Is that the standard you have set for yourself? Is that the way you live? As a person to whom God has given one of the highest places – and a person whom he has crowned with glory and honour?

But wait – there's more, check out the very next verses …

God Puts Me In Charge

> *You made them rulers over the works of your hands;*
>   *you put everything under their feet:*
> *all flocks and herds,*
>   *and the animals of the wild,*
> *the birds in the sky,*

> *and the fish in the sea,*
> *all that swim the paths of the seas (Psalm 8:6–8).*

'God has put everything under your feet.' Can you see what that means? Have you ever seen a wrestling match? One that is almost a fight to the finish? A match that keeps on going until one contestant is pinned helpless on the ground? How does the victor show that they have won? How do they demonstrate that they are superior?

They stand tall over their fallen competitor and place one of their own feet on top of them. It's a moment of victory. It's a moment of declaring who is in charge. That's what it means to place something *under your feet*. So – what has God placed under your feet? Look back at verse 6:

> *You made them rulers over the works of your hands;*
> *you put **everything** under their feet (Psalm 8:6, my emphasis).*

God has placed everything in all creation under your feet. You are in charge of everything God has created.

Who – me?

Yes, you!

Has God really placed *everything* under your feet? Read on …

Jesus Shows Me How To Be Free

If we look at Hebrews chapter 2 we'll see that the writer has obviously been reading Psalm 8.

Everything Under My Feet

> But there is a place where someone has testified:
>   'What is mankind that you are mindful of them,
>   a son of man that you care for him?
>   You made them a little lower than the angels;
>   you crowned them with glory and honour
>   and put everything under their feet' (Hebrews 2:6–8a).

We've already learned all that from Psalm 8. But if you were asking yourself: *'Has God really put* everything *under my feet?'* then the writer of Hebrews is asking the very same question! What does it mean that God has put *everything* under our feet? Read on …

> In putting everything under them, God left **nothing** that
> is not subject to them (Hebrews 2:8b, my emphasis).

Can you see how big your freedom is? God has made you to rule over everything, and there is *nothing* apart from God himself that you are not to rule over. Nothing? You mean I'm meant to rule over *everything?* Like, am I meant to rule over every *animal?*

Let's think about that. Are you meant to rule over the sharks? Could you take on a shark and win? Okay, if it's you versus a shark, one on one, and you're unprepared, then the shark might win. Or if it's you versus a lion, one on one, and you're unprepared, then the lion might just get the upper hand. But think about this: humans keep sharks in aquariums, sharks don't keep humans in aquariums. Humans keep lions in cages, lions don't keep humans in cages. God has designed you to rule over everything in his creation.

We Don't See Us In Control …
Everything? What about the *weather?* Are we meant to rule over it? Should you be able to say 'Today I command it to be sunny with no rain whatsoever?' I don't know about you, but I don't quite see humanity in control of *everything.* We talk about the weather. We complain about the weather. We get reports about the weather. We even make a stab at

predicting the weather. But we can't control it. In fact, we human beings aren't doing a great job of controlling much in the world at all. Look at the mess we keep making of our planet!

Now I know what you might be thinking:

> *'If I could have a say in how the world was run, it would be a better place. If I was in charge I'd do it better.'*

Or maybe you would find running the world a little daunting. Perhaps you'd just like more of a say in how your family is run. Or how your school is run. Or how your church is run. But it's not unusual to think: 'I could do a better job than the mob who is running it now.'

Could you? Would you really organise the world better? Can we do a quick check on that? Here's the key question: how are you doing at running the small bit of the world that you *do* have responsibility for? Even if you're a teenager, the place you probably have some control over is your bedroom. How are you getting on with running your own bedroom? If the world was organised the same way as your bedroom currently is, what sort of world would we live in? Not one of us is doing a very good job at running the bit of the world that we have responsibility for.

So what's gone wrong? Why do we not see the world being subject to us?

But We Do See Jesus

The next verse or two in Hebrews 2 answers this for us.

> '… [God] put everything under their feet.'
> In putting everything under them, God left nothing
> that is not subject to them. Yet at present we do not
> see everything subject to them. But we do see Jesus …
> (Hebrews 2:8–9a).

'But we do see Jesus …' We see Jesus being the human that we were designed to be. He is the one who rules God's world under God's authority. He is the one who stays on the rails and always puts into practice what his Heavenly Father wants. He is the truly free human being. Everything in creation is subject to him.

Can Jesus control the weather? Yes! He can say to the wind – 'Be quiet!' He can say to the waves – 'Be still!' That is the freedom that God created you to have. That is the person that God wants you to be.

So who is the real you? What are you really meant to be like? What is it that will fulfil the destiny that God has given you? You're meant to be just like Jesus. And anything that helps you become more like Jesus helps you to be really free. Anything that takes you away from becoming more like Jesus also takes away your true freedom.

People often think you've got to break away from God to be free. We think that somehow the 'real me' is just me doing whatever I want. We think that putting on Christian behaviour is not real, but false.

We think it goes like this:

The Real Me:
doing what I want

Being a Christian drags me away from being "me"

- The real me is the real sinful me
- Following Jesus takes me away from being real
- Following Jesus takes me away from being free

But here's the way it really is:

Being a Christian brings me back to being "me"

The Real Me:
designed by God to depend on him

- The real me is the me that God has designed me to be
- Following Jesus brings me back to my true freedom

Being a Christian helps take me back to what I'm really meant to be like. Growing as a Christian means I'm growing more and more free. It's sin that takes me away from being free. God wants you to really be free. God wants you to discover what he has done for you in a whole new way.

God wants you to rediscover the freedom that he gave you when he *first made* you. God wants you to rediscover the freedom that he restores in you when he *re-makes* you. God wants you to rediscover the absolute joy of becoming the person that he has designed you to be. God wants you to discover the real you. So that every person – everyone that you know – will look at you and discover the real Jesus.

That's what this book is all about. I pray that we will discover together how to be really free. I pray that you will discover how to be really you.

Let's go …

SECTION 2

Freedom Destroyed

Terminal Stupidity

An Infectious Disease

I want to warn you about an incredibly infectious disease that is spreading rapidly across the world at the moment. I'm worried. I see this ailment spreading from person to person and its effects are devastating. There appears to be no inoculation to prevent you from getting this sickness. And from my observation of those who have been afflicted with symptoms, there is no treatment. Once you get this disease, you appear to be stuck with it for life.

I am talking about the disease called Terminal Stupidity. I'm not referring to people who have disabilities. I'm not criticising people who have learning difficulties. I'm talking about the general population who appear to have been struck down with a devastating case of Terminal Stupidity.

Here are some actual cases that I have observed:

Case No. 1

We had a small flat in the backyard of our house. We wanted to turn it into my office, so we engaged a professional locksmith to install a deadlock. He showed up at our house with his little bag of tools, and disappeared down to our backyard flat to do his work.

An hour passed. Two hours passed. I thought I'd better check down there to see how things were going. As I approached the flat, I could see a brand-new shiny deadlock had been affixed to the door. And the keys were hanging on the outside.

Where was the locksmith? I heard a banging sound from inside the flat and a voice crying 'Let me out!' Our master locksmith had managed to install a new deadlock and then *lock himself in*. I thought to myself, 'A locksmith really only does two things in their profession. They install locks, and they pick locks. *How could this guy lock himself in with a lock that he himself had installed?*'

Terminal Stupidity.

Case No. 2

I went into a shop with my brand-new credit card. As I completed my purchases, the shop assistant asked me to sign the receipt. She then compared the signature on the receipt with the signature on my card. She announced to me: 'I can't authorise this purchase. Your signature on the receipt has to match the signature on your credit card. That's to prevent credit card fraud. I can't authorise your purchase because you haven't signed your credit card.'

I checked my card. It was brand new. I had forgotten to sign it. Oops! 'That's all right,' I said cheerily, 'I'll sign it now.' I promptly signed my credit card.

The shop assistant inspected my signature on the credit card and compared it with the signature on my receipt. 'It's okay. They match now.' So much for fraud prevention. Another case of Terminal Stupidity.

I now want to describe three scenarios to you. All of them are stupid. But I wonder if you would ever do them?

Would You Give Up Something Extremely Valuable For Something That Lasts For A Moment?

Imagine you have a million dollars, but you're really hungry and you've got the cravings for a Big Mac. You meet a guy who's just bought a fresh Macca's meal. You really want it. He offers to sell it to you for a million bucks. *Would you buy it?*

Would You Give Up Being Free To Become A Slave?

Imagine you are in a great family and your parents love you very much. It's a cool family with lots of fun and lots of purpose. You live in a great house, your parents are quite rich and generous. You have responsibilities, but you also have freedom. Would you leave that house and voluntarily go and live with a deranged criminal who treats you as a slave, tortures and destroys you? *Would you do that?*

Would You Give Up Your Whole Life For Instant Glory?

I heard of an athletics coach who was training athletes at world standard. He asked them: 'If I could give you a drug that could guarantee you a gold medal at the next Olympics, but would also kill you within six months, would you take it?'

Well, what would you say? Would you take it? Over half the athletes in his elite squad said *'Yes'*. Terminal Stupidity! Imagine giving up your whole life for temporary glory!

The Saddest Thing

But do you know the saddest thing about being a youth pastor for almost forty years? *I see students doing these things all the time.*

- Sometimes they give up something extremely valuable for something that lasts for a moment
- Sometimes they give up being free to become a slave
- Sometimes they give up their whole life for instant glory

I see students throwing away the most valuable thing they have – eternal life with God forever – because there's a sin they want to keep enjoying. I have seen guys walk away from Jesus because they want a fling with a girl.

I have seen young people give up the freedom they have in Christ. Maybe it's because they get hurt by someone at church, or God doesn't do exactly what they want, or they have a bad experience with their Christian friends. Whatever it is, they throw away the freedom that God has given them. They fall captive to their own sins, and they get involved in stuff which will eat away and destroy them. They leave the household of God, and their loving and caring father, and live with a spiritual slave-master who destroys them.

I have seen plenty of people throw away everything with God because they just want instant pleasure and glory now. I guess every time that you or I sin, that's exactly what we're risking. How could we do that?

All that freedom that we looked at earlier – being made free in God's image, being created by God to be a world ruler, being free to enjoy everything good, having God put everything under your feet, seeing Jesus to be the person that God has destined you to be – imagine giving all that away just for a moment of pleasure now. And yet you might well have a friend who has done just that. They looked like they were walking *with* Jesus but they ended up walking away *from* Jesus. Maybe right now you are feeling like you're right at that breaking point too.

I want to show you how easy it is to destroy the freedom that God has given you. I want to show you how three simple steps can take you away from every bit of freedom that God wants to give you. It might just be that you will need to take some drastic action to get back what you've given up.

Step 1 – Listen To The Temptation

In the next three chapters, I want to take you through three steps that Satan will use to try and get you to throw away the freedom that God has given you. These three steps have the potential to rob you of your future.

Here's the first step – *Listen to the temptation.* I want to examine the lies that the devil will throw at you to try and get you to destroy your freedom.

Let me take you back to where it all started. God gave amazing freedom to humanity when he created us in Genesis 1. But just two chapters later, Adam and Eve are on the verge of throwing the whole thing away.

Let's go up close and listen in …

Lie 1 – Doubt God

> *Now the snake was more crafty than any of the wild*
> *animals the LORD God had made. He said to the woman,*
> *'Did God really say, "You must not eat from any tree in*
> *the garden"?' (Genesis 3:1).*

The devil's first weapon is to get you to doubt what God has already said. 'Did God really say this? Surely he wouldn't say that, would he?'

Can you think of a time in your life when you really doubted God? I don't just mean asking questions about your faith. I don't just mean that there was something in the Bible that you couldn't quite figure out. Asking questions about God and the Bible can be very healthy, especially when it leads you to great answers!

But has there been a time where you started thinking that the whole thing wasn't true? Or that God didn't care about you? Or that God had let you down? That it wasn't worth even continuing as a Christian? Perhaps you were on the verge of giving up on Jesus altogether. Maybe you're feeling like that right now.

That's Satan's first weapon. If he can convince you to start doubting what God has promised, then he is well on the path to dragging you away from the glorious future that God has planned for you.

Once he has placed the seed of doubt in our minds, Satan moves on to Lie 2:

Lie 2 – Defy God

Eve answers the serpent:

> *The woman said to the snake, 'We may eat fruit from the trees in the garden, but God did say, "You must not eat fruit from the tree that is in the middle of the garden, and you must not touch it, or you will die"' (Genesis 3:2–3).*

Okay, she seems a bit confused when she adds 'and you must not touch it' – but basically, she gets it right. God had clearly said just one chapter earlier:

> *And the LORD God commanded the man, 'You are free to eat from any tree in the garden; but you must not eat from the tree of the knowledge of good and evil, for when you eat from it you will certainly die' (Genesis 2:16–17).*

This sounds pretty clear to me. Satan's next step is to flat out deny what God has said.

> *'You will not certainly die,' the snake said to the woman (Genesis 3:4).*

This is straight-out contradiction! God says: 'the day you eat of that tree – you will die.' The devil says: 'No, you won't!'

Satan does this all the time:

- God says, 'I want you to spend time with me today in my Word.'
- The devil says, 'It doesn't matter if you don't do it today.'

- God says, 'Things will go best for you if you tell the truth.'
- The devil says, 'Things will go worse for you if you tell the truth.'

- God says, 'Keep your sexuality for your marriage partner.'
- The devil says, 'What's the problem in trying it out now?'

What lie is Satan telling you that is the *exact opposite* of what God has already promised? Are you listening to the devil? Are you starting to believe him?

These are Satan's lies every time:

- Lie 1 – doubt God
- Lie 2 – defy God

Lie 3 – Discredit God

> 'For God knows that when you eat from it your eyes will be opened, and you will be like God, knowing good and evil' (Genesis 3:5).

Satan's next trick is to try and persuade you that God doesn't really care about you. That is, God can't be trusted.

> *'Come on – you don't really trust God, do you? He says not to eat of the tree of the knowledge of good and evil. He says it won't be good for you to do that. He says you will die. But what does he know? Come on, he's an old grouch, he knows that when you eat of the fruit your eyes will be opened and you will be just like him. He doesn't want that to happen. God is holding back something that would be good for you. Look at the fruit. It looks pretty good, doesn't it? God knows it will be fun, and that's why he's made up some stupid commandment to stop you doing it.'*

It's so easy to fall for that lie. To believe that God doesn't want the best for you. To think that he's holding something back that would be good for you. Every time you sin, you believe that lie. You believe that Satan is offering you a better deal than what God is offering you.

If you didn't believe that – you wouldn't sin.

A quick recap of Satan's lies:

- Lie 1 – doubt God
- Lie 2 – deny God
- Lie 3 – discredit God

Lie 4 – Deliver Nothing

*'For God knows that when you eat from it your eyes will
be opened, and you will be like God ...' (Genesis 3:5).*

Satan says: 'Do what I say and I'll let you become like God.'
Can you notice two rather suspicious things about this
promise, two things that make this a very bad deal?

He Promises Something That You Already Have

Remember what we learned in Genesis 1 – God has already
made us *in his own image.* Adam and Eve were already *just
like God.* This is an outrageous ploy by the evil one. *He
promises you something that you already have!* Don't fall for it.

He Promises Something That He Can't Possibly Give

Satan offers to make Adam and Eve just like God. Think
about that for a moment. Do you see the problem? *Satan
hasn't got the power to make them just like God!* Satan doesn't
have the power to make *you* become like God. He couldn't
do it if he tried for a thousand years. He offers to give you
something that he simply hasn't got the power to give.
And yet, we keep falling for it. Satan spins us the same
lie, 'Do it my way and I will give you satisfaction.' But
he hasn't got any satisfaction to give us. He is the most
dissatisfied being in the universe. Jesus has already given
us our satisfaction!

Satan's four lies:

- Lie 1 – doubt God
- Lie 2 – defy God
- Lie 3 – discredit God
- Lie 4 – deliver nothing

Why does he go to all this trouble? To get you to listen to him. That is the first step in your downfall. Because Satan knows that once you start listening to him, you are now ready for the second step in his fiendish strategy …

Step 2 – Carry Out The Sin

If you've already fallen for **Step 1** – and you've listened to Satan's lies, then he's got you ready for **Step 2** – where you *carry out the sin.*

Let me show you the dangerous road that this step will take you on. Let me explain to you how perilous it is to give in to Satan's temptations. Let me show you how the devil wants you to give up your freedom in four easy stages.

Stage 1 – Watch It

> *When the woman saw that the fruit of the tree was good for food and pleasing to the eye … (Genesis 3:6).*

Can you notice something? The woman's first step wasn't to grab a piece of fruit and shove it in her mouth. Her first step wasn't to defy God outright. Her first step was simply to *look* at it. She saw how mouth-watering it was. She observed how good it would be to bite into it. She contemplated how delightfully it sparkled in the sunlight.

She might well have been saying, 'Listen, I'm not going to eat it … I'm just going to look at it for a while. What's the harm in that? Wow! It looks good doesn't it?'

And we do the same thing. Satan says: 'Here's a sin that you'd really enjoy.' And our first step is to look at it. We imagine it. We picture it. And we say to ourselves 'I'm not going to do it, but wow! That sin looks like fun, doesn't it?'

Stage 1 sounds innocent enough. But if something is sinful, and you just claim: 'I'm only looking,' then you will quickly fall for Stage 2.

Stage 2 – Want It

> *When the woman saw that the fruit of the tree was good for food and pleasing to the eye, and also desirable for gaining wisdom … (Genesis 3:6).*

The more she looked at that fruit, the better it looked. The better it looked, the more she wanted it. The more she wanted it, the more she had to have it. The more she had to have it, the closer she got to taking it.

Has that ever happened to you? There is a temptation, you know it's wrong and you've decided that you're not going to do it. But you just look at it. You check out the details. You imagine what it would be like if you actually did it. You let the devil describe it to you. And the more you look at it, the more you want it. And you end up doing the very thing that you promised you would never do again. It's happened to me, and I'm sure it's happened to you.

- Can you see how the devil encourages us to turn temptation into sin?
  - Stage 1 – watch it
  - Stage 2 – want it

Stage 3 – Do It

> *When the woman saw that the fruit of the tree was good for food and pleasing to the eye, and also desirable for gaining wisdom, she took some and ate it ... (Genesis 3:6).*

That's how you end up giving up your freedom. When Satan presents a sin right in front of you:

- you watch it ...
- you want it ...
- you do it ...

How many times have you ended up doing the very thing that you were determined *not* to do simply because you followed these three easy steps. Each step seems so innocent in itself, that's why the devil's strategy is so clever. And as soon as you have reached Stage 3 – where you *do* it – it's not long before you start to drag others down as well.

Stage 4 – Drag Others Down

> *When the woman saw that the fruit of the tree was good for food and pleasing to the eye, and also desirable for gaining wisdom, she took some and ate it.* **She also gave some to her husband, who was with her, and he ate it** *(Genesis 3:6, my emphasis).*

Do you know one of the saddest things about sinning? You feel a whole lot better when you can get someone else to join in with you. You don't just drag yourself down, you drag your friends down as well.

Have you ever been with anyone while they are getting drunk? They're not happy until everybody else is getting drunk as well. Or have you ever seen somebody making fun of one of the other kids at school? The whole thing starts to snowball when other kids start joining in the ridiculing. It's almost as if sin can't stand being alone. It's not happy unless everybody is joining in.

And if you've ever ended up encouraging your friends to join in your wrongdoing, then you are doing the exact opposite of what Jesus wants you to do. He said: 'Go and make disciples of all nations. Go and help your friends follow me.' Wouldn't it be terrible if you were one of the reasons that your friend started *giving up* being a disciple?

I said there were three overall steps in destroying your freedom.

- Step 1 – Listen to the temptation
- Step 2 – Carry out the sin

There's one more …

Step 3 - Face The Consequences

Every choice has a consequence. If you choose to follow Jesus faithfully, then there are brilliant consequences for that. But if you follow the devil's path (**Step 1** and **Step 2**), then there is one more issue that you need to face, one more step that robs you forever of the freedom that God has planned for you.

- Step 1 – you listen to the temptation
- Step 2 – you carry out the sin
- Step 3 – you face the consequences

Look at what happened when the first human beings stepped away from the freedom that God had given them. Here are four consequences that nobody wants, but every time you sin, this is what you deserve.

Consequence 1 – Shame

Then the eyes of both of them were opened, and they realised they were naked; so they sewed fig leaves together and made coverings for themselves (Genesis 3:7).

What does 'they realised they were naked' mean? What! They realised it just then? You'd think they would've noticed before! I mean, I don't hang around a lot of naked people. I won't claim to be a world expert on this. But I think if the person who was standing right in front of me was naked – I'd notice it! I suspect they both knew that they were naked long before they sinned. So, what changed after they both had disobeyed God? Let's wind back to the previous chapter before Adam and Eve decided to sin:

Adam and his wife were both naked, and they felt no shame (Genesis 2:25).

Before they sinned, they felt *no shame*. But now they have sinned, they 'realised they were naked' and 'made coverings for themselves'. What has happened? They both feel *ashamed*. The first consequence of sin is *shame*. They are now ashamed of who they are in front of each other.

Guilt is like that. It always leads to shame. You know what you have done is wrong. You experience that feeling of shame. You would die if anyone else found out all the wrong things you've done. You carry that guilt with you.

And one of the consequences of carrying that guilt is shame. Deep down, you might well feel guilty about what you have done. Deep down, you might also feel ashamed of who you are. Guilt is when you feel bad because of *what you have done*. Shame is when you feel bad because of *who you are*.

Consequence 2 – Fear

> *Then the man and his wife heard the sound of the* Lord *God as he was walking in the garden in the cool of the day, and they hid from the* Lord *God among the trees of the garden. But the* Lord *God called to the man, 'Where are you?'*
> *He answered, 'I heard you in the garden, and I was afraid because I was naked; so I hid' (Genesis 3:8–10).*

The second consequence of sin is fear. Up until they sinned, Adam and Eve had had a perfect relationship with God. They would chat with him face-to-face. Their relationship was honest and open. But now they are guilty, what do they do when they hear the sound of God in the garden? They hide! They're scared to face God. They run away because they know they are guilty.

Guilt is like that. It brings fear into a relationship. I'm sure that there are some occasions when you just don't want to face up to God. You know that sometimes you will hide from him. There will be instances where you don't want to open your Bible and read it, because you don't want to hear what God says. You're scared that if you listen to him, things will have to change in your life. When you know you feel guilty, you will always feel afraid.

- Consequence 1 – shame
- Consequence 2 – fear

Consequence 3 – Blame

When you feel guilty, you want to offload some of that guilt onto someone else. You start playing the blame game. From Adam and Eve through to Bart Simpson and Judge Judy … everyone is blaming someone else.

> But the LORD God called to the man, 'Where are you?'
> He answered, 'I heard you in the garden, and I was afraid because I was naked; so I hid.'
> And he said, 'Who told you that you were naked? Have you eaten from the tree from which I commanded you not to eat?'
> The man said, 'The woman you put here with me – she gave me some fruit from the tree, and I ate it.'
> Then the LORD God said to the woman, 'What is this you have done?'
> The woman said, 'The snake deceived me, and I ate' (Genesis 3:9–13).

God says to the man: 'Why did you eat the fruit?'

Adam answers: 'It wasn't my fault – it was her! In fact, God, it was the woman *you* put there.'

God says to the woman: 'What have you done?'

Eve answers: 'It was the snake's fault.'

We do it all the time. When we feel guilty, we'll do anything to shift the blame to someone else. We blame everyone, except ourselves.

- Consequence 1 – shame
- Consequence 2 – fear
- Consequence 3 – blame

Consequence 4 – Separation

> And the LORD God said, 'The man has now become like one of us, knowing good and evil. He must not be allowed to reach out his hand and take also from the tree of life and eat, and live for ever.' So the LORD God banished him from the Garden of Eden to work the ground from which he had been taken. After he drove the man out, he placed on the east side of the Garden of Eden cherubim and a flaming sword flashing back and forth to guard the way to the tree of life (Genesis 3:22–24).

Guilt separates you from God. It separates you from God's paradise. It separates you from God's blessings. It separates you from God's freedom.

Adam and Eve destroyed the freedom that God gave them. They had a perfect relationship with God where they met face-to-face in total trust. They had a perfect relationship with each other where they were completely open in front of each other without shame. They had a perfect relationship with their environment where they lived in a garden paradise. They had a perfect relationship with themselves, they had the freedom to be the people that God had created them to be.

- They destroyed their perfect relationship with God
- They destroyed their perfect relationship with each other
- They destroyed their perfect relationship with their environment
- They destroyed their perfect relationship with themselves

Their freedom had turned to guilt. It's the same when you defy God – *your* freedom turns to guilt. And guilt is a burden that will crush you. No one can survive bearing the extreme weight of their sin. It weighs you down. It drags you back. It keeps you under pressure. It crushes you.

Your fragile human body, your vulnerable emotions and your raw feelings were never designed to carry around this burden of guilt. Your body was designed to be free, to carry with you the freedom that God has given to you. Your body is designed to be in a perfect relationship with God, with others, with the world and with yourself.

Your *body* was never designed to be weighed down by the burden of your guilt. Your *emotions* and your *personality* were never designed to be weighed down by the burden of your guilt. *You* were never designed to be weighed down by the burden of your guilt. When you are carrying your own guilt, every part of you is affected.

Maybe you are busting your chops to be acceptable to your parents, but you're never quite good enough and you're weighed down with more guilt. Perhaps you have been criticised so much, and are feeling so guilty, that if anyone even has the slightest criticism of you it hits you like a tonne of bricks. You either get really upset by it, or you defend yourself with, 'how dare anyone else criticise me!' Maybe you've just snapped at someone you love, or exploded in a tantrum, or gone off to sulk. Perhaps you've given up on school, on friends, even on Jesus. If you're guilty in one area of your life, every part of your life is affected.

If you've been involved sexually in a way that you know you shouldn't, you feel that guilt, and you might go around absolutely condemning anyone else who ever fails in that area. You might do anything you can to try and get rid of your guilt. But guess what? Nothing works. You can't do anything to actually get rid of it. Our only hope is if somehow every bit of our guilt can be taken away and dealt with once and for all, forever. Maybe this is the time when you will discover what God has done for you in a way that you never realised before.

What are you currently involved with that is destroying your freedom? What temptations are you listening to? What sins are you carrying out? What consequences do you now have to face? What will you do about that guilt that is crushing you? Is this the moment where you know that things simply have to change?

SECTION 3

The Need To Be Freed

The Problem Of Guilt

Have you ever been trapped, and no matter what you did you couldn't break free?

I remember when I was a little kid at school. I was just a 5-year-old, and there were some big 7-year-olds who were real bullies. They often picked on me. One day, when I was in the boys' toilet at school, these bullies locked me in. They were all bigger than me, and they stood outside the door and pushed so hard that I couldn't open it. There was no way out. My life flashed before my eyes. To me, it felt like I might have to spend the rest of my life inside those school toilets. The situation was crushing me, and no matter what I did, I couldn't break free.

Maybe you have also experienced, or are experiencing, a situation where it feels that there is no way out. You might feel absolutely trapped or stuck in the middle. No matter what you do, you just can't fix it. It might be that your parents are breaking up and you desperately want to stop them. You try to engineer things at home to make it happy families again. You think that maybe you're the cause, so you aim to be the perfect kid for as long as you can. You try to say things that will fix it all up, but the more you say, the worse it gets. The situation you're in is crushing you – and you can't break free. Perhaps it's something completely different. But you wouldn't be human if you didn't feel trapped at some stage of your life.

We've been looking at feeling trapped in the Bible. It's what happens when you ignore what you know is right ... and do what you know is wrong ... when you refuse to do things God's way ... and you just do things your own way ... when you give up the freedom that God has designed for you ... and you take on the guilt that you know you deserve ... and you become trapped by guilt. You know it's crushing you but you cannot break free. When you're guilty, you feel terrible. Guilt eats away at you and starts to affect many areas of your life.

Your guilt lies beneath so many of your failures, so many of your bad experiences and so many of your relationship breakdowns. Your guilt tears away at your relationship with God, your relationship with others, and your relationship with yourself.

Nobody can stand this. We all try to get rid of it somehow. Here are the six most popular ways that most of us use to try and ease the pain of guilt:

1. Justify It

One way to try and ease your guilt is to convince yourself that it wasn't wrong in the first place. Perhaps you can make up an excuse to try to explain away that what you did wasn't really that wrong at all. You've always got a reason; you've always got an excuse; you can always talk your way out of anything. Maybe some of the feelings of guilt will die down for a short time, *but your actual guilt still remains*.

2. Blame Others

This is one of the most popular methods around. If you've done the wrong thing, just blame somebody else! Kids blame their brothers or sisters; husbands blame their wives; workers blame their bosses; coaches blame their players; children blame their parents; Adam blamed Eve; Eve blamed the serpent; everybody blames somebody else!

> *'It's Jimmy's fault. He broke the window. He ducked out of the way when I threw a brick at him.'*

But it doesn't work. Maybe some of the feelings of guilt will die down for a short time, *but your actual guilt still remains*.

3. Criticise Others

One popular method of dealing with feeling lousy about yourself is to try to make everyone else feel worse than you. Do you know someone who is constantly critical – always finding fault with everything you do? My suspicion is that they feel guilty and they don't know how to deal with it. When you see someone else who's got the same fault as you have, it's tempting to be very critical of them. It's easier to criticise the fault in someone else, rather than trying to fix it in yourself. It still doesn't work, *your actual guilt still remains.*

4. Cover It Up

You know how this works. Perhaps you are playing with a ball inside your house, despite the fact that you have been told not to. You accidentally crack your mum's treasured vase – so you simply turn the vase around so no one can see the crack. The great cover up. Or maybe you sipped some alcohol from a bottle in your parents' cabinet at home, and then put some water in the bottle to cover up what you did. Some people live their whole lives this way. And constantly trying to cover up more and more to protect your image is exhausting. Even if you're successful, you might dodge some of the consequences, *but your actual guilt still remains.*

5. Try And Make Up For It

Think of a time when you've hurt someone by saying the wrong thing or doing the wrong thing by them. What did you do to try and restore the relationship? Sometimes you can try to make up for it by doing endless good deeds for them. You buy them things, you help them around the house, you do anything they say to try and make up for your guilt. As every parent knows, if you want someone to be your slave for life, then never forgive them. Because if you can keep them feeling guilty before you, they will do whatever you say. Some parents keep their children feeling guilty their whole lives. What a burden that must be! You can try to make up for the wrong stuff you have done, the trouble is, it doesn't work. *Your actual guilt still remains.*

6. Become Religious

> 'God – if you get me out of this mess, I'll become a missionary in some third world country for the rest of my life!'

Sometimes we think that if we do lots of things for God, it will somehow make up for the bad stuff we have done. When you stand before God on judgement day, and he asks: 'Why should I let you into heaven?', some people will be tempted to answer: 'Because I put up with all those boring church services for twenty years!' Some young people go to their Christian youth group and come forward at every altar call without ever having their life turned around. All because they're feeling guilty.

When you sin, you are in debt to God's laws and you are in debt to God. Your sins are like debts that you owe, so as you continue to sin, this inbuilt 'debt-collector' goes to work. You look for a way to pay off your debts, but you can never do it. No matter how many good things you do, you can never make up for all the bad things you have done. No matter how many times you try to impress God, you will still feel guilty.

Living with guilt is an intolerable burden. Nobody can live like that. Guilt is the most oppressive slave-master that you could ever be subjected to. Most of us will do anything to try and get rid of those horrible feelings of guilt. The trouble is, all of these methods might make some of your *feelings* of guilt die down, *but your actual guilt still remains.*

Surely there's a way forward? The good news is that there is! The bad news is that it might get worse before it gets better ...

10

The Nine Spiritual Terrorists

Even if you get to the point where you think you're getting a bit better, there's always something that drags you down. Did you realise there is a whole squadron of enemies who are trying to defeat you and keep you enslaved to your guilt? I want to warn you about nine spiritual terrorists who are there trying to drag you down at every opportunity.

A terrorist is someone who uses violence and intimidation to get the result they want. Terrorists don't care who they hurt – they don't even care if they hurt themselves. And they work behind the scenes – if you're not watching, you don't even realise they are the enemy. When those innocent commuters boarded those flights back on 11 September 2001, they didn't know who the terrorists were. Those Australians holidaying on the island of Bali, didn't know who the terrorists were either.

If you go along in your Christian life unaware of who the spiritual terrorists are ... if you're not alert to those forces in the universe that are trying to tear you away from Jesus at every opportunity ... if you don't know who your enemies are and how they will try and keep you enslaved to guilt all your life ... then you run the risk of having your Christian life blown away. You risk having your Christian life torn to pieces. You face the threat of surrendering your freedom to slavery forever.

I want to identify each of these spiritual terrorists and then show you how each of them will try to keep you as a slave to stop you enjoying the freedom that God has designed for you.

1. Sin

Jesus replied, 'Very truly I tell you, everyone who sins is a slave to sin' (John 8:34).

Sin is like a master who wants to control you. Every time you give in to sin, you let sin control you just a little bit more. So, the next time you're tempted by the same sin, having already given over a little bit more control, you're much more likely to sin again. You become even more enslaved, which means that the next time you sin, you give more control away until you're controlled so much by sin that you feel you can never escape.

Once, when I was a young boy, my older sister and I were in the supermarket together. She handed me a packet of sweets and told me to put them under my jacket so we could get away without paying for them. I was horrified! I had never done anything like that before! I was terrified that we would be caught, but we got away with it. The next time my sister and I tried to pull the same stunt, it was easier. We felt more comfortable with it. We were becoming slaves to that sin.

Come on, you feel like that with some of your sins don't you? You've fallen for them so many times that you feel you can never escape.

If somehow you could deal with your guilt, then sin would have no more power over you.

2. Law

Did you know that inbuilt into every human being is the need for laws? We might resent the laws, we might hate the laws, we might break the laws, but we cannot live without laws. Even when there are no laws, we make them up for ourselves. Did you ever make up rules when you were a kid? You would be happily walking along the footpath – where there were no rules whatsoever. Then somebody would make up a rule. Like, 'you're not allowed to walk on a crack in the pavement', and for the rest of the journey you would have to walk in obscure and convoluted ways to avoid breaking this new 'rule'.

I see guys in our youth group throwing a ball around. It's not a competition. It's just a bunch of guys having fun. But pretty quickly, someone makes up a rule, 'Before you catch the ball you have to clap.' Then another quickly follows, 'If you miss the ball you have to do six push-ups.' All in good fun. We have such a need for laws that even when there are none, we will make some up.

Laws are good things. They might annoy you sometimes, but basically, they are helpful things. They are guidelines to get us through life. Laws are like lane markings on a road. They keep all the traffic flowing smoothly and safely. Imagine if there were no lane-lines, people could drive wherever they liked. It would be chaos! The rules might be difficult to obey sometimes, but laws are good for us.

God's laws are good too. They show us what is right and wrong. They guide us through the complexities of life. They show us what God's character is like. They show us how to please God. God has given them to us as a sign of his love for us. But here's the problem, we are powerless to obey God's laws. God's laws *show* us what is right, but they do not give us the power to *do* what is right.

Most of us think: 'If I can just obey God's laws I will be right with him.' But have you ever tried to be 'good'? Have you ever decided: 'I'm not going to disobey God ever again?' Have you ever made a promise like: 'I'm never going to commit that sin again in my life?' Do you see the problem? Because you know you *must* obey – and yet you *don't* obey – you are paralysed by guilt. And every time you break one of God's laws, you stand condemned by that very law. You are enslaved by that law.

> *... the sinful passions aroused by the law were at work in us, so that we bore fruit for death. But now, by dying to what once bound us ... (Romans 7:5–6).*

The Bible says that you were held captive by God's laws. Every time you disobey one of God's laws, that law stands there to condemn you and remind you that you are guilty before God.

If somehow all your guilt could be dealt with, then God's law would no longer have any hold over you.

3. Condemnation

> *The wrath of God is being revealed from heaven against all the godlessness and wickedness of people, who suppress the truth by their wickedness (Romans 1:18).*

People of all civilisations fear the anger of God. That's why across the world, in every culture and in every century, people have devised religions where they have to do various tasks and rituals to appease their angry God.

When you know you're guilty, you don't want to face God. When you don't want to face God, you are in constant dread of the time when you have to stand before him and give an account of your life.

If you were no longer guilty, then you would have no problem facing up to God.

4. Satan

> *Be alert and of sober mind. Your enemy the devil prowls*
> *around like a roaring lion looking for someone to devour*
> *(1 Peter 5:8).*

Satan knows you are guilty before God. He is on solid ground when he stands there and accuses you day and night. Satan reminds you of how you've failed God and of how guilty you are and suggests: 'You may as well give up on Jesus.' Sometimes we do.

If you were not guilty in the first place, then Satan would have no power over you.

5. Demonic Powers

Sometimes we tend to think that Satan is just operating all alone, sort of like a very dark spiritual Rambo. You need to remember that he has a whole evil spiritual army at his disposal. He has an entire network of spiritual terrorists who will look for any opportunity to drag you down.

> *For our struggle is not against flesh and blood, but against*
> *the rulers, against the authorities, against the powers of*
> *this dark world and against the spiritual forces of evil in*
> *the heavenly realms (Ephesians 6:12).*

Do you see how Satan's demons are described? 'The rulers … the authorities … the powers of this dark world … the spiritual forces of evil ...' Along with Satan, they will use any opportunity to drag you down, remind you that you are guilty, and try to rob you of the freedom that God wants you to have.

If you were not guilty in the first place, then the demons would have no power over you.

6. Your Own Desires

What do we do about all this? Some Christians say: 'If we can hide away from the world, then we can escape the spiritual terrorists who will try and drag us down.'

Back in the Middle Ages, some Christians built giant monasteries with huge walls to keep all the 'bad' things and 'bad' people out. People became monks and lived in these monasteries their whole life so that they never had to come into contact with those 'sinful' people out there. But each one of those monks took a spiritual terrorist in with them:

> For it is from within, out of a person's heart, that evil thoughts come – sexual immorality, theft, murder, adultery, greed, malice, deceit, lewdness, envy, slander, arrogance and folly. All these evils come from inside and defile a person (Mark 7:21–23).

Your own evil desires will tempt you, lead you to sin, tear you down, hold you enslaved and multiply your guilt. Sin is not like a sickness that you might catch if you mix with the wrong people. Sin is like death, it is inbuilt into your own body. You could lock yourself alone in a room for the rest of your life and you would have as much sin in there as a person on the outside world.

Your sin comes from within you, to hijack you and destroy you. Your own desires are spiritual terrorists that will try and keep you enslaved to guilt. Somehow all that guilt has to be taken away so that you are no longer held captive by your own desires and so that you can regain the freedom that God designed you to have.

If you were not guilty in the first place, then your desires would have no power over you.

7. Conscience

… a guilty conscience … (Hebrews 10:22).

Everyone has a conscience within them that tells them right from wrong. It is a very valuable guide because it helps to show you how to live. But when you fail to live up to the standard of your own conscience, it becomes a terrible tyrant. Your conscience can be a spiritual terrorist that will condemn you for your failures. You can ignore your conscience, but you can't silence it. Even if you lower the standards in your conscience, you will still fail your new lower standard. While your guilt remains, your conscience drags you down.

If your guilt could be removed, your conscience would have no more power to condemn you.

8. The World

> *We know that we are children of God, and that the whole*
> *world is under the control of the evil one (1 John 5:19).*

The Bible says that the whole world is under the control of Satan. He has deceived us all. Everything about how our world operates is affected by sin and opposed to God.

Living in this sinful world is like standing on a backwards-moving escalator. You can't stand still. You will be dragged down. If you sometimes feel like it's a bit of a struggle to hang in there as a follower of Jesus, then that's perfectly understandable. God says the whole world is trying to drag you down. The whole world is a spiritual terrorist who tries to keep you enslaved to your own guilt.

If somehow all your guilt could be effectively dealt with, once and for all, then the world would have no more power to drag you down.

9. Death

> *… by his death he might break the power of him who*
> *holds the power of death – that is, the devil – and free*
> *those who all their lives were held in slavery by their fear*
> *of death (Hebrews 2:14–15).*

Everyone is scared of death at some stage. No one normally looks forward to dying. It's the topic that no one wants to talk about. Most of us avoid the idea at all costs. We try to protect ourselves from even thinking about death. We do all sorts of crazy things to live longer, live with less pain, live healthier and to avoid the onset of death at every opportunity. And yet it's the one thing that you know you can't prevent. You can't stop it. We are not the masters when it comes to death. With all our modern medicine and hi-tech hospitals, we like to pretend that we're in charge of this death stuff. But we're not in control. We're not even close.

When you die, you have to face up to God. But if all your guilt could be dealt with, death would have no fear for you.

How on earth will you survive with all that guilt and with those nine spiritual terrorists trying to drag you down all the time?

Surely God will just forgive us. Um … won't he?

Will God Always Forgive?

Right now, you might be breathing a sigh of relief because you're saying to yourself, 'At least God always forgives me. Everyone knows that. I've been taught that since I was a little kid. God forgives everyone's sins.'

I mean, that's what God does, doesn't he? That's his job. He forgives sins. It's sort of automatic. It's part of his job description. It's like a McDonald's employee asking, 'Would you like some fries with that?' It's part of their job description. It's like a teacher saying, 'Have you done your homework?' Or a librarian saying, 'Shhhh'. It's all part of their job description. God is like that, isn't he? God forgives sins. That's his job, isn't it? Or is it?

Is Forgiveness Automatic?
Let's check out a few key passages from the Bible:

> *The* LORD, *the* LORD, *the compassionate and gracious God, slow to anger, abounding in love and faithfulness, maintaining love to thousands, and forgiving wickedness, rebellion and sin.* **Yet he does not leave the guilty unpunished** ... *(Exodus 34:6–7, my emphasis).*

This passage from Exodus describes the God who forgives wickedness, and it includes the words 'Yet he does not leave the guilty unpunished ...' Interesting:

> *Let us examine our ways and test them,*
>   *and let us return to the* LORD.
> *Let us lift up our hearts and our hands*
>   *to God in heaven, and say:*
> *'We have sinned and rebelled*
> **and you have not forgiven'** *(Lamentations 3:40–42, my emphasis).*

Did you notice it? This cry to God in Lamentations includes the sentence: 'We have sinned and rebelled and you have not forgiven.'

Listen to the words of God himself:

> **'Why should I forgive you?**
>   *Your children have forsaken me*
>   *and sworn by gods that are not gods.*
> *I supplied all their needs,*
>   *yet they committed adultery*

and thronged to the houses of prostitutes.
They are well-fed, lusty stallions,
    each neighing for another man's wife.
Should I not punish them for this?'
    declares the LORD.
'Should I not avenge myself
    on such a nation as this?' *(Jeremiah 5:7–9, my emphasis).*

Are you getting the idea that God's forgiveness is not automatic?

Surely these things happened to Judah according to the LORD's command, in order to remove them from his presence because of the sins of Manasseh and all he had done, including the shedding of innocent blood. For he had filled Jerusalem with innocent blood, **and the LORD was not willing to forgive** *(2 Kings 24:3–4, my emphasis).*

If you've gained the impression over the years that God just automatically forgives sins, you could not be further from the truth. These passages make it clear – God does not routinely forgive every sin. So, what *does* God think about your sin?

Your eyes are too pure to look on evil;
    you cannot tolerate wrongdoing *(Habakkuk 1:13).*

God can't just forgive sin. God is holy. He is totally separate from evil. His holiness burns so brightly that he consumes and destroys evil. If you approached God with one tiny little bit of sin on you, you would be consumed and destroyed by the fire of his holiness.

It's like trying to land a space expedition on the sun. No matter how good your space programme is, the sun burns with such a fierce intensity that as soon as you got anywhere near, you would be consumed by the burning fire of the sun. In the same way, if you try to approach God with one tiny little bit of sin on you, you would be consumed and destroyed by the burning fire of his holiness.

God is holy. Sin is ugly. God cannot just forgive sins. He can't just sweep it under the carpet. His holiness and his purity demand that he treats it with the utmost importance.

Is There Any Way Forward?

Right in the middle of all this, God talks about a day where he will do something absolutely incredible for us:

> *I will sprinkle clean water on you, and you will be clean; I will cleanse you from all your impurities and from all your idols. I will give you a new heart and put a new spirit in you; I will remove from you your heart of stone and give you a heart of flesh. And I will put my Spirit in you and move you to follow my decrees and be careful to keep my laws (Ezekiel 36:25–27).*

God says there is a day coming that will change everything:

> *On that day a fountain will be opened to the house of*
> *David and the inhabitants of Jerusalem, to cleanse them*
> *from sin and impurity (Zechariah 13:1).*

If you've sort of gone along thinking your sin doesn't really matter ... if you've just presumed that God will forgive you anyway ... if you've thought that somehow when you face up to God, hey – it'll be sweet ... then maybe today you have to rethink your life big time. God says our sin really does matter. God is holy – he hates our sin. You can't just waltz up to God and pretend that nothing has ever happened. The only way you can ever stand before God – and survive – is if every bit of your guilt has been absolutely dealt with.

In the next section, I want to show you what God has done so that every speck of your guilt can be done away with forever. I want to show you from the Bible how you can regain the freedom you have lost. If you have never come to Jesus to have your sins dealt with, then I want to show you how you can say 'Yes' to the magnificent gift that Jesus is offering you.

Welcome ... to your day of freedom!

SECTION 4

The Day Of Freedom

12

This Is A Big Deal

There are some things in life which can seem like really *little* things at first – but you quickly discover they aren't that little at all – they become a really, really *big* deal.

This happens all the time in boy/girl relationships. Guys continually think that something they've said or done, or something they *haven't* said or done, is really no big deal. But to the girl it is often a big, big, big deal.

The guy forgets the three-month anniversary of their first date. To him it's no big deal. 'It's just a number on a calendar.' But to his fair lady, this is a *big* deal. By forgetting the date, she feels like he is forgetting *her*.

The girl says to her guy, as she pats his bulging biceps, in a voice of solid admiration: 'My man is putting some powerful kilograms on!' He replies, 'You're looking pretty fat yourself.' Ouch! It's so easy to think that something is no big deal, but in reality, it's a big, big deal.

Maybe someone said something insulting to you. They thought it was just a joke. They laughed it off. But it hurt you. It *really* hurt you. They thought it was *no big deal*. But to you, it really mattered.

It Really Matters!

Wouldn't it be terrible if there were something that you treated as *no big deal*, and you found out, way too late, that it *really* mattered? Something that you dismissed as irrelevant but you later discover that your whole life depended on it.

It's very easy to think about Jesus' death that way. Ever since you were a little kid, you've heard, 'Jesus died on the cross', 'Jesus died to save you from your sins', 'Jesus died to forgive you.' The trouble is that you've heard it so many times it's lost most of its meaning. It doesn't seem like a big deal. Jesus is God. He can do anything. So why shouldn't he die on a cross? He knows he's going to rise again. What's the big deal?

I'm not suggesting you don't believe it. You probably believe every word of it. But you've just heard it too many times. You know how the story ends. It doesn't surprise you. It doesn't shock you. You're kind of glad it happened; it's just that it's not a big deal.

I want to set the stage so you will see how the death of Jesus is an enormously *big deal*. It's not just something that Jesus did to fill in time one lazy afternoon. The journey that Jesus takes to the cross is one that God had planned since the very beginning. Jesus' death and resurrection was one of the biggest events in the whole of human history, and it is one of the biggest displays of power that could ever occur in your life.

Let's Just Backtrack For A Minute

God has designed you to be free. He made you to be just like himself. He handcrafted you to be a world ruler – so that you would help run this planet his way. His plan was that you would be free in your relationship with him, free in your relationship with others and free in your relationship with yourself.

Every time you sin, you eat away at the freedom that God designed for you. Every time you sin, you become more of a slave to sin. And that wrecks everything. It wrecks the freedom you have in your relationship with God, in your relationship with others and in your relationship with yourself.

You trade your freedom for guilt. Your guilt weighs you down and you feel ashamed. You feel afraid. The burden of your guilt is difficult, and you start to blame everyone else. No one can live with guilt in their body. But there is absolutely nothing you can do to get rid of it. Every time you think you might just be getting ahead, there are nine spiritual terrorists who will try and drag you down at every opportunity.

God is holy. Your sin is ugly. God cannot just forgive sins. He can't just sweep it under the carpet.

There Is Hope For All Of Us

Right now, I want you to experience the death of Jesus in a bigger way than you have ever experienced it before. My prayer is that the enormity of what God did on that day as he shattered the course of humanity will sink into you in a way that it never has before. Wouldn't it be brilliant if you could see how *big* a deal it was when Jesus Christ hung on that cross on that day?

On that day, God changed the eternities of thousands of generations. Every evil force in the universe was defeated. Every spiritual terrorist was annihilated. On that day, every barrier between you and God was demolished. The slavery of your guilt was destroyed. God gave you your freedom back. God's own Son fought for and won the greatest victory that has ever been achieved so that your life could be changed forever.

God achieved that day of freedom *then* so that you could achieve your day of freedom *now*. On that day, on that cross, Jesus changed everything. So that on *this* day, at *this* moment, you can make a decision that changes everything.

Maybe today, on *this* day, you will realise that you have never seen Jesus' death as a big deal in your life. Maybe today God will prompt you to say *'yes'* to Jesus in a way that you never have before.

You know you need a day of freedom. Maybe for you – today will be that day.

13

Jesus On Trial

I want to take you back to a day that changed the world. Come with me to around the year AD 30. We're now in the nation of Israel. But the Israelites are not running their own nation. The Romans invaded some years before, and the Israelites are second-class citizens in their own country. Even though Rome holds all the positions of power, they have allowed the Jewish religious leaders, the Pharisees and the teachers of the law, to take charge of religious matters. As well as the official Roman army, there are also temple guards which the Romans allow to have a small amount of authority.

In this nation of Israel, come with me to a small garden just outside the capital city of Jerusalem. A man known as Jesus of Nazareth has been rising in popularity over the past few years. Many are following him, but the Jewish leaders are opposed to him. In the garden of Gethsemane, the Jewish leaders are about to strike. They want to take Jesus down – and end his ministry forever.

By reading all four gospels, and by placing them in chronological order, I want to walk you through the sixteen hours that changed the world. In less than one day, the world will be transformed. This is your day of freedom.

The events are accurate. The specific times are estimates based on the biblical evidence. The sixteen hours that will change the world are about to commence late one Thursday evening. If you want to read the original records for yourself; here's where you'll find them:

- Matthew 26:36 – 27:66
- Mark 14:32 – 15:47
- Luke 22:39 – 23:56
- John 18:1 – 19:42

Come with me, it's late on a Thursday night and Jesus is praying in a garden …

Late Thursday Night – The Arrest

Jesus falls to his knees in prayer. At the very moment that he needs the support of his disciples, they fall asleep and leave him alone. He sees the horror of what lies ahead, and his sweat is like drops of blood falling to the ground.

It's now around midnight. A crowd of armed guards show up to arrest Jesus. One of Jesus' closest friends, Judas, has turned against him. He is one of Jesus' twelve disciples whom Jesus has lived with, loved and taught for the past few years. He betrays Jesus with a sign that usually signifies a very close friendship, he kisses him. But this is no act of love. This is an act of treachery. This is a signal for the guards to pounce. Jesus is tied up and led away. Within one hour he will face his first trial.

1:00 A.M. Friday – Trial 1, Annas

At about one in the morning, Jesus is interrogated by Annas, one of the two high priests. When they don't like the answers Jesus gives, they slap his face. Annas does not find Jesus guilty, but keeping him tied up with ropes, he sends him off to Caiaphas, the other high priest.

2:00 A.M. Friday – Trial 2, Caiaphas

Jesus' second trial with Caiaphas is much longer and stretches over three hours. It starts at about two in the morning and goes on until after daybreak. False witnesses are paid to bring evidence against Jesus, but their stories are confused and don't agree.

There is only one thing they can find Jesus guilty of – blasphemy. That is, claiming to be the Son of God. But can you see that if he really *is* the Son of God, he has just been convicted of telling the truth? His only 'crime' is to be truthful.

Those in the interrogation chamber spit on Jesus. They blindfold him and take it in turns to hit him with a lump of timber. They yell out at him, 'If you're such a prophet, then tell us which one of us hit you.'

As Jesus leaves, he sees his best friend Peter across the courtyard. If ever there is a time where he needs Peter to stand by him, it is now. But as he looks at Peter, he knows that his best mate has just deserted him. His friend Peter, who vowed he would never leave him, has just shouted out for the third time, 'I never knew the man!'

Even though Jesus is not guilty of any real crime, Caiaphas has decided that Jesus should die. But they need the Roman Court to enforce the death penalty. So, after being grilled for three hours by Caiaphas, Jesus is hauled off to his third trial before the Roman governor, Pontius Pilate.

5:30 A.M. Friday – Trial 3, Pilate

Pilate interrogates Jesus but finds no fault in him. Pilate concludes, 'I find no reason to condemn this man.' But the crowd is calling for Jesus' death. Pilate thinks he sees a way out. He discovers that Jesus is from Galilee. Pilate knows that King Herod rules that region, so Jesus is bundled off to trial number four.

6:00 A.M. Friday – Trial 4, Herod

It's now around six in the morning. Jesus was arrested around midnight. He has had no sleep. So about six hours after his arrest, Jesus is now facing his fourth trial.

Herod wants to see some miracles, but Jesus chooses not to perform any signs. Herod also isn't able to find any guilt in Jesus, but, together with his soldiers, he ridicules and mocks Jesus. He then ships Jesus back to Pilate, for his fifth and final court appearance.

6:30 A.M. Friday – Trial 5, Pilate (again)

It is only seven hours since Jesus has been arrested, it is still early on Friday morning, but Jesus is facing his fifth consecutive trial. He is back before the governor, Pilate.

Eventually Pilate gives his verdict, 'he has done nothing to deserve death.'

But Pilate has a problem. The crowd is crying out for Jesus' death. They are threatening to report Pilate to Caesar if he does not convincingly deal with him. Pilate tries to see if they will allow him to release Jesus, but they choose for the convicted criminal Barabbas to be released instead. Finally, Pilate gives in. Even though he has found Jesus to be totally innocent, he orders him to be whipped and then executed by crucifixion.

14

Jesus Is Tortured

7:00 A.M. Friday – The Whipping

By this stage, Jesus would have been exhausted. He had been praying with great fervour in the garden before being arrested. Then he was put through five separate trials throughout the small hours of the morning, he was hit around and slapped on the way, but not one court found him guilty of any real crime. He is an innocent man, but he is about to be put to death.

But before the cross, he is sentenced to a Roman whipping. The Romans were experts at designing torture for their victims. They were the most feared army in the world. So even though Jesus had been sentenced to death, Pilate ordered for him to first be tortured.

The Roman guard would have had a whip with many different thongs of leather attached. Each piece of leather was long enough to wrap right around a man's body. And along each of these leather thongs, they would tie in various bits of sharp metal and rock at intervals along the whip. This means that as the whip landed on the victim's body, each piece of sharp metal or rock would bite into the victim's skin, tearing the skin, and exposing a bloody sore. This was not only excruciatingly painful as these bits of metal and stone dug deep into the victim's skin, but imagine the agony when the guard flicked the whip back out, and every one of those sharp implements tore away a small amount of flesh.

To prepare him for the whipping, Jesus had been stripped naked. His hands were tied above his head and his feet were anchored to the ground. He received thirty-nine lashes. He was whipped all the way from the back of his neck right down to his feet. And each leather thong was long enough to wrap around his entire body. There was not one part of his flesh that was not exposed and torn to shreds.

It has been estimated that by the time Jesus had finished being whipped he would not have had a piece of unbroken skin on him any larger than a coin. His whole body would have been a bleeding mess. The pictures that artists have painted of him across the years have been tidied up because if you had witnessed the actual mess of bleeding, gaping flesh that covered Jesus, you would have turned away in horror.

The Roman whipping was sometimes referred to as 'the first death' because many prisoners did not survive this harsh and barbaric treatment. But against all odds, Jesus survives.

And now the soldiers decide they will have their own fun with Jesus.

8:00 A.M. Friday – The Crown Of Thorns

Jesus is led away by the soldiers who want to make fun of him. They mock him for claiming to be a king. They spit on him and they hit him. They find a purple robe to wrap around him. They place a staff in his hand. They mock him by pretending to worship him. The soldiers think that this 'king' needs a crown, so they gather together some giant thorns, and twist them together into a crude crown. They place this on Jesus' head. They probably hit the crown of thorns into his scalp. And each thorn would have drawn more blood and caused more pain.

There's one last act just to increase the agony more. The robe they had placed on him would have had time to congeal to his mess of bleeding wounds. They then rip the robe off him – and no doubt reopen every one of Jesus' painful sores. Then they lead him away to be crucified.

8:30 A.M. Friday – Jesus Carries His Cross

Jesus is now forced to carry his cross to outside the city wall where he will be executed. His cross is heavy and Jesus is weak and feeble. He falls under its weight as it crushes him down. A passer-by, named Simon, is ordered to help him carry his execution machine.

After all this, Jesus finally arrives at the one moment that would change everything.

Jesus Is Killed

9:00 A.M. Friday – Jesus Is Hung On The Cross

Jesus now arrives at his place of execution, Golgotha – the place of the skull. His cross is laid on the ground and Jesus lies down, face up, with his arms outstretched on top of it. One Roman guard stands on his arm, another stands on his hand, a third grabs a Roman nail – somewhat like a tent-peg – and drives it into Jesus' wrist. The nail pierces him between his radius and his ulna. This has to support his weight. He is firmly nailed into the timber cross.

Then his other arm is nailed, and then his feet. Then the cross is raised upright – ready to be lowered into the hole that will keep it secure. The cross is dropped into this hole, and Jesus' body jars as it sags with the weight.

An innocent man is being executed. In five separate trials he was not found guilty of any real crime. He has been shamefully treated. Whipped to within an inch of his life, stripped naked and humiliated as he hangs on a cross like a common criminal. What is his attitude to these wicked men who are perpetrating such an injustice? He looks at his attackers, and cries out in prayer, 'Father forgive them …'

Amazing.

Crucifixion is an excruciatingly painful method of execution. Most societies that use capital punishment have devised a method that is quick and painless so that it will cause a minimum of distress to the criminal and to the onlookers: hanging; beheading; firing squad; electrocution; lethal injection. As horrifying as these methods of execution are, they all have a common theme, they will cause death quickly and painlessly.

The Romans had devised crucifixion as the most horrible way for a person to die. They reserved this vilest of execution methods for the Jews, whom they despised. Indeed, if you were a Roman citizen, and you were sentenced to death, you were not allowed to be crucified. You would be beheaded – which is quick and painless. The torture of crucifixion was kept aside for the people the Romans hated most, the Jews.

Death by crucifixion is painful and slow. When you are suspended by your arms, it gets harder and harder to breathe. That's because your diaphragm gets weaker and weaker. Your diaphragm is the large muscle that pushes your lungs up and down. If you've ever been 'winded' when you've been hit in the stomach – and you found that you couldn't breathe – that's because your diaphragm was knocked out of alignment for just a second. Imagine it getting weaker and weaker, so that every breath becomes harder and harder to take. That's how you die by crucifixion. Slowly, hour by hour, until you eventually asphyxiate.

As they were struggling for breath, prisoners on the cross would try to push themselves upwards with their legs to take the pressure off their arms. Just for a moment, so they could take one more breath. Then they would sink down in agony again. Then they would struggle to push themselves up with their legs, and so it went on, slowly and painfully, until they drew their last breath.

That's why the Romans would sometimes come and break the legs of the prisoners who were hanging on the cross. This might be seen as cruelty, but in reality, it was an act of kindness – because it brought on their death more quickly. The criminals who were crucified on either side of Jesus had their legs broken. But when they came to Jesus, they did not break his legs. He was already dead. Just to make sure, one of the soldiers rammed his spear through Jesus' ribs, and blood and water flowed out – showing that Jesus had definitely died.

Crucifixion is terribly slow, and terribly painful and terribly agonising. The Bible records that Jesus was placed on the cross at nine in the morning and that he did not die until three in the afternoon. Six long hours. And during the heat of the day, he was taunted by the crowd to prove he was the Son of God by freeing himself from such a painful death, which he could have done. But he chose to stay there because he did not have his *own* freedom in mind. He had *your* freedom in mind.

3:00 P.M. Friday – Jesus Dies

This was no ordinary day. The author of life was being put to death. The Lord of the universe was being regarded as trash on a rubbish heap. The perfect, righteous and holy Son of God was being treated like a common criminal. The creator of all was being crushed to death. If you had been watching, you would have sensed that something big was happening. The Bible records that from midday until three in the afternoon darkness fell across the land, as the universe was being turned inside out on this fateful day.

But that was nothing compared with what happened in the universe at the *moment* that Jesus died. The Bible passage is below, because if you didn't see it for yourself, you would think I was making it up. Extraordinary events happened at the moment that the Lord of life was put to death:

And when Jesus had cried out again in a loud voice, he gave up his spirit. At that moment the curtain of the temple was torn in two from top to bottom. The earth shook, the rocks split and the tombs broke open. The bodies of many holy people who had died were raised to life. They came out of the tombs after Jesus' resurrection and went into the holy city and appeared to many people (Matthew 27:50–53).

This is amazing stuff. Imagine trying to make a movie about all this!

Here's what happened at the moment that Jesus died:

The Curtain Of The Temple Was Torn In Two

The curtain in the temple separated the 'holy of holies' from the rest of the temple. Only the high priest was allowed to enter – and only on very special occasions. The curtain was designed by God to show that sinful human beings could not approach a holy God. It separated us from God, it blocked our access to him. As the curtain of the temple is torn in two, it shows us that by Jesus' death we are now granted access into the very throne-room of God. No longer do we need to remain separate, because of Jesus' death, you now have full access to God the Father.

And why does it matter that it was torn *from top to bottom*? It was a huge, heavy curtain. If it were torn by humans, it would have been torn from *bottom to top*. The fact that it is torn from *top to bottom* shows that it is God himself who is breaking down the barrier that keeps us from his presence.

The Earth Was Torn In Two

'The earth shook and the rocks split.' Can you imagine it? The whole planet rumbles with anticipation at the moment Jesus dies.

Graves Were Torn In Two

> *... the tombs broke open. The bodies of many holy people who had died were raised to life. They came out of the tombs after Jesus' resurrection and went into the holy city and appeared to many people (Matthew 27:52–53).*

Can you picture that? Graves open up and dead people come back to life! Because of Jesus' death, there is now no more barriers between the living and the dead. Death will be conquered when Jesus rises in just three more days.

This is unbelievable stuff! Jesus' death is a *big, big deal*. Not only is the planet being torn in two at the death of this remarkable man, but also the *whole of humanity* will be torn in two by this extraordinary moment.

And if everything you've read so far is not enough to set your mind boggling, check out *what else* the death of Jesus achieves for you.

Well, go on – turn to the next chapter!

16

Every Enemy Is Defeated

You could not get a more significant or powerful event in all of history. On that day, Jesus not only surrenders his freedom for yours; Jesus not only takes the ugliness of your sins from you; Jesus not only takes every one of your sins and failures and deals with them decisively; but on that day, on that cross, Jesus defeats and completely overpowers every one of the nine spiritual terrorists who might try to stop you regaining your freedom.

Let's check out what happens to each of those nine spiritual terrorists:

1. Sin

*For we know that our old self was crucified with him so that the body of sin might be done away with, **that we***

> *should no longer be slaves to sin … (Romans 6:6, my*
> *emphasis).*

On that day, on that cross, Jesus smashed the power of sin so that you no longer have to be enslaved by it.

2. Law

> *… He forgave us all our sins, **having cancelled** the charge*
> *of our legal indebtedness, which stood against us and*
> *condemned us; **he has taken it away, nailing it to the***
> ***cross** (Colossians 2:13–14, my emphasis).*

On that day, on that cross, Jesus smashed the power of God's law to accuse you and condemn you so that you no longer have to be enslaved by it.

3. Condemnation

> *Therefore, **there is now no condemnation** for those who*
> *are in Christ Jesus, because through Christ Jesus the law*
> *of the Spirit who gives life has **set you free** from the law*
> *of sin and death (Romans 8:1–2, my emphasis).*

On that day, on that cross, Jesus took the condemnation that you deserved. He smashed the fear that you stand condemned before God so that you no longer have to be enslaved by it.

4. Satan

> *The one who does what is sinful is of the devil, because the devil has been sinning from the beginning. **The reason the Son of God appeared was to destroy the devil's work** (1 John 3:8, my emphasis).*

On that day, on that cross, Jesus smashed the power of Satan to bind you up in the slavery of guilt so that you no longer have to be held captive by him.

5. Demonic Powers

> *And having **disarmed the powers and authorities**, he made a public spectacle of them, **triumphing over them by the cross** (Colossians 2:15, my emphasis).*

In those days, when a king conquered another kingdom, he would capture the defeated king, and all his officials, and all his generals, and all his soldiers, and all his people – and tie them up in a long chain and parade them back down the main street of his home town. This is so his own people could see that every one of their enemies had been captured and were now disarmed. They would never cause them any problems again.

That verse in Colossians 2 shows how at the cross Jesus disarmed the devil and his legions of demons, and led them in a victory parade to show that his people never need to be enslaved by them again.

On that day, on that cross, Jesus smashed the power of the demonic forces so that you no longer have to be held captive by them.

6. Our Own Desires

Those who belong to Christ Jesus have crucified the flesh with its passions and desires (Galatians 5:24).

On that day, on that cross, Jesus takes all your sinful desires and he puts them to death on that cross. The power of your sinful desires to hold you captive has been done away with forever.

7. Our Conscience

*… let us draw near to God with a sincere heart and with the full assurance that faith brings, having our hearts sprinkled to **cleanse us from a guilty conscience** … (Hebrews 10:22, my emphasis).*

On that day, on that cross, Jesus takes your guilty conscience. He removes all your sins, smashes all your guilt and takes away all your condemnation. He totally cleanses you from your guilty conscience so that it can no longer condemn you and hold you captive as a slave to your guilt.

8. The World

> '... I have overcome the world' (John 16:33).

On that day, on that cross, Jesus smashed the power of the world to drag you down and take you away from him so that you no longer have to be enslaved by it.

9. Death

> ... but it has now been revealed through the appearing of our Saviour, Christ Jesus, who has **destroyed death** and has brought life and immortality to light through the gospel (2 Timothy 1:10, my emphasis).

On that day, on that cross, and through his mighty resurrection, Jesus smashed the power of death so that you no longer have to be enslaved by it. By dying, and then rising from his tomb three days later, Jesus demonstrated for all time that the final enemy of death had been totally defeated. Jesus' death could not hold him down – and now *your* death cannot hold *you* down. Because Christ has risen triumphantly from the grave, he can now offer you eternal life so that your day of freedom can last forever.

On that cross, and at his resurrection, Jesus destroyed everything that could keep you away from enjoying the freedom that God has designed for you. He smashed every spiritual terrorist who would try to drag you back to your life of shame. He demolished every spiritual terrorist who would try to drag you back to your life of fear, your life of blame and your life of guilt.

When you become a Christian, on that cross Jesus becomes *you* in the sight of God. He bore in his body on that tree all *your* filth. Every bit of sin which should have destroyed you – Jesus took it!

The separation from God that you should have experienced – he experienced. The death which you should have died – he died. God's judgement fell on him instead of on you. The anger of God was poured out on him instead of on you.

So, for the Christian, there is nothing of you: your sin, your guilt, your fear, your inferiority, your shame, your deceit, your resentment, your bitterness, your hatred, your hurt, your bondage, your idolatry, your insecurity, your selfishness, your disobedience, your emotional traumas, your mental torments, your rage, your sexual misconduct, your self-despising.

All this was taken away at the cross. There is nothing for which Christ did not take up into himself on that cross, pay the penalty for, destroy, and totally wipe away forever.

At the cross God saw you at your worst, and loved you the most. Christ wiped away everything, all your sin, and all your guilt, and all your punishment. He paid for the lot himself.

It's done. By Jesus you can be made clean. You can be forgiven. You can have every sin totally wiped away.

And your eternal life? Jesus achieved that for you when he rose from the dead. He now offers it to you as a free gift. Jesus has won your freedom and he wants you to have it for keeps. All you need to do is say 'yes'. To say 'yes' with your lips; to say 'yes' with your heart; and say 'yes' with your life.

I don't know where you stand at the moment. Maybe you have been a faithful Christian for years, and you're now seeing Jesus' death in a much bigger and grander way. Or maybe you were *sort of* a Christian, but you know you have not stuck to the path that Jesus has created for you and maybe right now you need to come back. Or it could be that you have *never actually given your life to Jesus* and you know that now is the time to do it.

How do you make the change to become a genuine Christian?

Read on!

17

Your Heart Surrendered

How do you make the change to become a genuine Christian? How do you take on board the freedom that Christ has won for you? How do you break free from your guilt and your sin so that you are now unleashed to live the life that Christ has designed for you?

Can I suggest three steps that will help you?

- Confess Jesus with your lips
- Believe Jesus with your heart
- Trust Jesus with your life

Here is the Bible passage that I am basing this on:

> ... *if you declare with your mouth, 'Jesus is Lord,' and believe in your heart that God raised him from the dead,*

you will be saved. For it is with your heart that you believe and are justified, and it is with your mouth that you profess your faith and are saved. As Scripture says, 'Anyone who believes in him will never be put to shame.' For there is no difference between Jew and Gentile – the same Lord is Lord of all and richly blesses all who call on him, for, 'Everyone who calls on the name of the Lord will be saved' (Romans 10:9–13).

Let's check it out.

Confess Jesus With Your Lips

*… if you **declare** with your mouth, 'Jesus is Lord,' and believe in your heart that God raised him from the dead, you will be saved. For it is with your heart that you believe and are justified, and it is with your mouth that you **profess your faith** and are saved (Romans 10:9–10, my emphasis).*

You need to talk to Jesus. You need to have a heart-to-heart conversation with him. You don't need any fancy words, you don't need any special formulas, you simply need to cry out to him in prayer. You can pray it out loud or you can say it silently. You can pray it by yourself or say it with a friend. But if you want to enjoy the freedom that Jesus has won for you, then you need to start a conversation with him.

What do you say? I will leave that up to you. But here is a suggestion:

- Tell Jesus that you are sorry for all your sins
- Ask Jesus to forgive you of every sin through his death and resurrection
- Commit your life to following him no matter what

Well, go on! If you're ready, talk with Jesus in prayer. Maybe it's time for you to make the most important decision that you will ever make in your whole life. If you're ready to commit your life to Jesus, put this book down, and go and do some serious business with God.

Back so soon? Let's check out the next step that goes hand-in-hand with the first one:

Believe Jesus With Your Heart

> ... *if you declare with your mouth, 'Jesus is Lord,' and* **believe in your heart that God raised him from the dead***, you will be saved.* **For it is with your heart that you believe and are justified***, and it is with your mouth that you profess your faith and are saved (Romans 10:9–10, my emphasis).*

You can't just say meaningless words to Jesus. You have to believe them in your heart. There is no magic prayer that will make you into a Christian. If you say words to Jesus, even if it is the best prayer ever created, but you don't mean it, then your words mean nothing.

You know what it's like when people make promises to you and then don't follow through with action? In the end, their words are meaningless. And meaningless words … well … they mean nothing!

You can't just ask Jesus for forgiveness and then go on your merry way with nothing ever changing. If you're confessing with your lips that 'Jesus is Lord', then you must also 'believe in your heart that God raised him from the dead'.

And if you genuinely believe this with your heart, the third step will follow straight on:

Trust Jesus With Your Life

As Scripture says, 'Anyone who believes in him will never be put to shame' (Romans 10:11).

Your lips must confess that Jesus is your Lord, and your lips need to be backed up by the belief of your heart. And your heart needs to be backed up by living a whole new life that shows you trust Jesus.

So, right now, what needs to change in your life if you're going to be serious about following Jesus? Are there things that you're currently doing that you know you need to stop? Or are there things that you are currently *not* doing that you know you need to start? If you are genuine about wanting to submit your life to Jesus, then you need to back that up with a life that is changing. That's what the Bible calls *repentance*. You turn away from doing what is wrong, and you start doing what is right. Not just once. Not just for today. But for every day of your life. Growing as a Christian is a life-long commitment!

But How Do I Know God Will Accept Me?
Good question! The rest of the passage from Romans 10 will answer that for us:

> *For there is no difference between Jew and Gentile – the same Lord is Lord of all and richly blesses all who call on him, for, 'Everyone who calls on the name of the Lord will be saved' (Romans 10:12–13).*

It doesn't matter whether you come from a Christian family or a non-Christian family. It doesn't matter whether you currently go to church or whether you've never been to church. It doesn't matter whether you've been a fine upstanding citizen, or whether you're one of those people who ends up in trouble all the time. It doesn't matter whether you are a Jew or a Gentile.

If you genuinely confess Jesus with your lips; if you genuinely believe Jesus with your heart; if you genuinely trust Jesus with your life; then the promise of God holds true for you: *you will be saved*. Jesus' death and resurrection have set you free. You are a brand-new person and Jesus is calling on you to start living a brand-new life. If you are genuine about giving your life to Jesus, then your day of freedom has arrived. Your day of freedom starts now. Your day of freedom will guide you for eternity.

But don't try to live for Jesus all by yourself. When you come to Christ, you join his community of faithful believers. There's a whole stack of other Christians just waiting for you to link up with them so that they can walk with you every step of the way so that no one ever gives up.

Are you already linked in with a church or a Christian youth group? Then go and talk with the leaders of that group so that they can help you. Do you have a friend or family member who goes to a church or Christian youth group? Then talk to that person, and go with them.

Christ has died and risen again so that you might be free. You now have a whole life to live enjoying that freedom that God has designed you for. So how should you live now that you are free to obey?

SECTION 5

Free To Obey

18

A Crazy View Of Freedom

Imagine there's an elite sporting team that you're desperate to get into. This is a national team so you'd get to represent your country at the top level in your chosen sport.

You train hard for a year. You sacrifice your own luxuries to reach peak performance. You go through the agonising selection of the try-outs. You push yourself to the limit. The coach himself comes down to check you out. When the coach issues the final team list – *your name is on it!* You are so excited! You've been chosen for the top team – you're in! You are the envy of all your friends!

So what do you do now? On the first training night, you go and set fire to the team's training equipment, then you slash the tyres of the coach's car.

'*What are you doing?*'
'*It doesn't matter now. I'm in the team. I don't have to impress the coach any more. I'm free to do what I like.*'

That's crazy! The coach chose you to be on the team to help the team achieve their best. You weren't chosen to be on the team so you could trash the coach's car!

Imagine another scene. (This is addressed to the guys. Girls – just reverse everything!)

There's a girl – and she's *hot*. And you think to yourself 'This is the girl for me!' So you woo her. You give her attention. You pay her compliments. You buy her flowers. You take her to cool places. You sweep her off her feet and lavish her with attention. Then, to make your relationship official, you ask, 'Will you be my girl?' She smiles sweetly and immediately replies, 'Yes!' This is what you worked for. This is what you put in all that effort to achieve. This is the ultimate result you hoped for. You two are now *an item*.

So what do you do now? You stop going where she wants to go and you just drag her along to what *you* want. When she comes over, you ignore her, and invite your mates over to watch the cricket on TV. You belch and you fart. You slob about in trackies, making no effort with your appearance. When she says, 'Honey – we need to talk,' you snarl back, 'Woman get back in the kitchen and bring me another snack.'

'Why are you treating her so badly?'
'She says she's my girl. I don't have to impress her any
more. I've got what I'm after. I'm free now. I can treat
her any way I want.'

That's crazy! She didn't agree to be your girl so you could treat her badly. She agreed to be your girl so you would keep caring for her the way you did when you first met.

One more scene, picture this:

You want to follow Jesus, but you feel weighed down by your own guilt. Every time you try to obey God, you fall flat on your face. You're desperately trying to do what is right, but you keep failing time and time again.

Then you discover that Jesus has died for you. You discover that Jesus has set you free. You discover that Jesus has dealt with absolutely every bit of your sin and every bit of your guilt. He's made you his. He's placed you on his team. He's entered into a personal relationship with you. You know you are forgiven. You know you've been made clean.

So what do you do now? You know that you're definitely a Christian, you're *in*, so you just keep on sinning. You don't care about obeying God. You don't bother changing those things in your life that you know are wrong. You don't care if what you do is hurting God. You don't care if you trash him.

'What on earth are you doing?'
'Jesus has set me free from my sins. I know I've been

forgiven. Now that I'm a Christian, it doesn't matter what I do. Jesus has already picked me – I don't have to obey him anymore. Jesus has died for me. God will forgive me. God has set me free. I can now do what I like.'

That's crazy! Jesus didn't die for you just so you could keep on sinning. Jesus didn't set you free so you could use your freedom as an excuse to do whatever you want. Jesus didn't put you on his team so you could trash him and abuse him and treat him like dirt. He put you on his team so that your life could be changed forever, so that you could be holy, so that you would now honour him in everything that you do.

God has called you to be free. 'You, my brothers and sisters, were called to be free' (Galatians 5:13). But God did not call you to be free so you'd be free to keep sinning. God called you to be free so that you'd be free to obey him.

So how do you do that? How do you live out your freedom?

Three Ways To Live Your Freedom

We've already seen that God calls us to be free in Galatians 5.

> *You, my brothers and sisters, were called to be free (Galatians 5:13).*

So – how do you live out that freedom? If we read on in Galatians 5, there are three clear steps that God gives us. Let's look at the first:

1. Feed The Right Thing

Don't Feed Your Sinful Nature ...

> *You, my brothers and sisters, were called to be free. But do not use your freedom to indulge the flesh (Galatians 5:13).*

It's so easy to think, 'I've been set free by Jesus – I can now do what I like – it doesn't matter if I sin.' But that's not why Jesus set you free! Yes – you've been called to be free. But don't use your freedom as an excuse to live in sin.

You know there's a sinful nature lurking in you. You know you're going to have wants and desires that are wrong. God says, don't give in to this. Don't follow this. Don't feed this.

What does it mean to *not feed* your sinful nature? Feeding something means giving it anything that will cause it to grow. If you've got pimples and you eat lots of fatty food, then you will feed your pimples and they will grow. If you've got a beer gut and you feed your beer gut with lots of fast food and lots of beer, then it will grow. If you've got a cute little kitty and you feed it lots of good things like milk and cat food, then it will grow into a nice big cat.

Feeding something is giving it anything that will cause it to grow. So, what does 'don't feed your flesh' mean? To put it simply: don't give your sinful nature anything that will cause it to grow.

If you get tempted to look at pornography then you feed that sin every time you look at a web page that you're not meant to. When you feed that sin, it grows within you. If you get tempted to tease other people and make fun of them, then you feed that sin every time you put someone else down or hassle them. When you feed that sin, it grows within you. If you're tempted to gossip about people and talk behind their back, then every time you listen to gossip and every time you pass on a rumour you are feeding that sin. When you feed a sin, it grows within you.

The Bible says: 'Do not use your freedom to indulge the flesh' (Galatians 5:13); don't 'gratify the desires of the flesh' (Galatians 5:16). To summarise all this, God is saying to you: 'Don't feed your sinful nature.'

Jesus did not die on the cross and set you free so you can feed your sinful nature. He did not die on the cross so that you could become more selfish or look at more pornography or ignore him at every opportunity. Jesus did not die on the cross and set you free so you could keep on sinning.

So don't feed your sinful nature. There is an alternative – *starve it to death!*

Starve It To Death!

> Those who belong to Christ Jesus have crucified the flesh
> with its passions and desires (Galatians 5:24).

The alternative to feeding your sinful nature is to crucify it! You nail your sinful nature to Jesus' cross. You put to death that sinful nature within you.

'But how do I do that? My sinful nature is so strong. I don't know how to "put it to death"!' I understand what you mean when you say that. Sometimes I feel the same way. But here's an idea: if you want your sinful nature to die within you – starve it! If you starve it of food, it will not grow and it will start to die. If you do not put fuel in the engine, then you will not be dragged along by it.

Jesus did not die on the cross and set you free so you can *feed* your sinful nature.

Jesus died on the cross and set you free so that you can put your sinful nature to *death*. And you put it to death by *starving* it.

When I was a very young Christian, I used to swear a fair bit. I used words that degraded God, and words that degraded other people. I don't think I *meant* to do anything particularly wrong. I had just slipped into the habit of using these words. I used them without thinking. I had fed my habit and my habit had grown. After some close Christian friends challenged me on this, I could see the damage I was doing with my language. I was hurting other people and I was hurting God, so I decided to change the way I spoke.

Did I change overnight? No. But every time I deliberately did *not* use a swear word, I *starved* that part of my sinful nature. And the more I starved it, the more it died. Forty years later, that part of my sinful nature is *so starved* to death now – I hardly ever even *feel* like using a swear word. It is no longer part of my nature. It has died.

Think about the sins that you find difficult. I simply want to ask, are you *feeding* that sin or are you *starving* it? If you're feeding it, then it will grow. But if you're starving it, then it will die.

It's like taking two dogs for a walk on two separate leads – one in each hand. One dog races off to the right; the other races off to the left. You're in the middle – holding both leads – struggling not to be ripped in two. If this happens every day, which way will you end up being pulled? Which dog will become the stronger dog? It depends on which one you *feed* ... and which one you *starve*.

So there's Step 1: feed the right thing. Now, let's read further into Galatians 5 and check out Step 2:

2. Build The Right Relationships

Don't Destroy Others ...

> *If you bite and devour each other, watch out or you will be destroyed by each other (Galatians 5:15).*

Do you know how easy it is to have a go at someone else? Do you know how easy it is to tease someone else? Do you know how easy it is to snap angrily at someone else?

> *If you bite and devour each other, watch out or you will be destroyed by each other (Galatians 5:15).*

Jesus didn't die on the cross and set you free so you can call other people names. Jesus didn't die on the cross and set you free so you can push other people around, or criticise them, or point out their failures, or tear them down at every opportunity.

It must break Jesus' heart when he looks down and sees

two Christians who can't get on with each other. How it must hurt him to see us being sharp with each other. How it must distress him to see us being rude to each other. How it must offend him to see us making fun of each other. You could imagine Jesus saying: 'I smashed down every barrier so that you could be united together as my people. How come you're putting up those barriers again and attacking each other?'

The good news? There is an alternative to destroying others:

Serve Them In Love

> *You, my brothers and sisters, were called to be free. But do not use your freedom to indulge the flesh; rather, serve one another humbly in love. For the entire law is fulfilled in keeping this one command: 'Love your neighbour as yourself' (Galatians 5:13–14).*

Jesus died on the cross and set us free to call us into a community. Jesus died on the cross and set us free to call us into rich and real relationships with each other, to call us to serve one another in love.

How do I do that?

> *For the entire law is fulfilled in keeping this one command: 'Love your neighbour as yourself' (Galatians 5:14).*

Hmm. The golden rule. You've heard that before. But have you ever worked out what 'To love your neighbour as yourself' means?

You might well think, 'I don't love myself.' I can understand why you would feel that, but can I suggest that you probably do love yourself. Indeed, I *hope* you love yourself!

What do you do if you fall over and graze your arm? You look after your wound, and you care for your arm. That's how you love yourself. So, what should you do if your *friend* is hurting? You should love them the same way that you would love yourself by looking after their hurt and taking care of them.

What do you do when you're tired? You rest. That's how you love yourself. So, what should you do if your *friend* is tired? You should love them the same way that you would love yourself. You should do anything that is needed so that they can rest.

What do you do when you're hungry? You feed yourself. That's how you love yourself. So, what should you do if your *neighbour* is hungry? You should love them the same way that you would love yourself. You should feed them because they matter to God and they matter to you.

Jesus did not die on the cross and set you free so that you could push everyone else around and have your own way. Jesus died on the cross and set you free so that you could serve others in love.

As we keep reading in Galatians 5, check out Step 3:

3. Walk The Right Way

Don't Walk Away From God's Spirit …

> *For the flesh desires what is contrary to the Spirit, and the Spirit what is contrary to the flesh. They are in conflict with each other, so that you are not to do whatever you want (Galatians 5:17).*

God's Spirit is pulling you in one direction. Your sinful nature is pulling you in the other direction. The Bible warns you, 'don't walk away from God's Spirit.' So right now, if God is calling you to obey him in some particular way, then don't walk away from him. There is an alternative:

Keep In Step With God's Spirit

> *Since we live by the Spirit, let us keep in step with the Spirit (Galatians 5:25).*

Do you know what it means to *keep in step* with someone? It means that you follow their movements exactly. It means that you go where they go and you do what they do. That's what it means to keep in step with them.

On one of our camps, our Year 12s put on a special concert item to say farewell as it was going to be their last camp as students. The whole cohort performed a brilliantly choreographed dance. Now I know these Year 12s. Many of them are not the world's best dancers. So how did they end up all doing the same dance steps together?

I watched carefully. And then I worked it out. They had placed one of the Year 12 students out in front of the whole chorus line. This guy was a *brilliant* dancer. Everybody else got all the dance moves right because they all watched the guy at the front. They stayed in step with him. They followed his moves exactly, and by staying in step with him, everybody got it right.

This is how you keep in step with God's Spirit. You keep in step by watching God's Spirit closely, by following his movements exactly and by going where he goes and doing what he does. Jesus did not die on the cross and set you free so you could walk away from his Spirit. Jesus died on the cross and set you free so you could keep in step with his Spirit.

If Christ has set you free, then you are now free to obey him.

20

Neither Do I Condemn You ...

Fear And Hope

Apparently, there are only two emotions that motivate humans to action. One is hope – and the other is fear. Advertisers know this and so many ads will either fill us with hope, 'You can have a sparkling clean kitchen that is the envy of all your neighbours.' Or their ads will fill us with fear, 'What if one of your own children got sick because your kitchen was dirty?'

Most people have worked out that if you want instant results, go for *fear*. When people feel guilty and afraid they will do almost anything to get themselves out of trouble. Parents, schoolteachers and sporting coaches will often use fear as an immediate motivator. 'You will be grounded ... you'll be put on detention ... you'll miss out on being selected for the team.' We all use it because we know it works. If you can make someone feel *guilty* enough, or *fearful* enough, you can probably make them do almost anything.

But it doesn't last. Fear only works for a short time. Eventually you resent it and you rebel against it. The problem with fear is that it never builds a relationship you want to stay in. If the only reason a child obeys their parents is because they're scared of being punished, then that will never build a solid family. If an employee only works hard because they're scared of getting sacked, then they will never achieve their potential. *Fear* might get instant results, but by itself, it destroys relationships.

Some people become Christians primarily because of fear. They don't want to go to hell. They don't want to be judged by God. Some people obey God mainly because they're afraid. They don't want to end up on the wrong side of someone who is all-powerful. And while there is a rightness about having a reverent awe or fear of a holy God, can you see that if fear is the *only* reason a person stays as a Christian, then there is something vital missing from their relationship with Jesus?

If the only reason that a person follows Jesus is that they're scared of being punished by him, then that is not the relationship that Jesus would ever want with anyone. It's like me saying to you: 'I want you to become my friend – otherwise I will hit you across the head repeatedly.' If you only become my 'friend' so that I won't hit you, then we don't really have a genuine friendship at all.

And yet, some people live their whole lives as 'Christians' out of fear. They miss the fact that the whole reason behind Jesus coming and dying for us was to wipe away that fear. He came to fill us with hope. And *that's* the relationship that Jesus wants with you.

So far ... so good.

Love And Justice

Here's the problem: as soon as someone finds out that God is no longer *angry* at them; as soon as they discover that every sin has been *forgiven;* as soon as they realise that any sin they commit in the future will be forgiven because Jesus has already died for them some people conclude: 'It doesn't matter if I keep sinning. It's already been forgiven. God really doesn't mind.'

I want to take you to an incident in the life of Jesus that shows that every sin can be forgiven, and that how you live from this point on *really matters*.

We're heading to the beginning of John chapter 8. A woman has been brought before Jesus because she has been caught red-handed in the act of adultery. This was not just a sin against God, in those days, it was also a crime against the state. The people were still operating on the laws that God had given when he was forming the nation of Israel, including that the sin of adultery was punishable by death.

They accuse this woman, not because they have any desire to uphold God's law or because they have any concern for the woman at all, but simply to test Jesus. They want to know what he will say. If Jesus says, 'Yes – enforce the law – she must be stoned to death,' then where is his love? But if he says: 'No – ignore the law – she should be spared,' then where is his justice?

In dealing with this tricky situation, Jesus wants firmly to display *both* God's love *and* God's justice. And as he does that, he says something very powerful for each one of us.

Let's listen in as this hostile crowd confronts Jesus:

> The teachers of the law and the Pharisees brought in a woman caught in adultery. They made her stand before the group and said to Jesus, 'Teacher, this woman was caught in the act of adultery. In the Law Moses commanded us to stone such women. Now what do you say?' They were using this question as a trap, in order to have a basis for accusing him (John 8:3–6).

Jesus knows their motives. He can see that they don't love God's law. They certainly don't love the woman. Jesus can see straight through their hypocrisy. Can you spot the immediate problem? They had brought the *woman* to be judged by God's law, but where was the *man*? Had he escaped scot-free?

The whole crowd is already standing there with rocks in their hands and with their arms raised ready to dispense instant justice. Everyone listens as Jesus, the rabbi, makes his pronouncement:

> 'Let any one of you who is without sin be the first to
> throw a stone at her.' (John 8:7).

Jesus didn't say that *everybody* had to be without sin. Only
the *first* person to throw a stone. Presumably, once that
person had started, everybody else could join in. Once
someone could prove that they were more righteous
than this woman, more righteous that anyone else in the
world, they were entitled to commence God's judgement.
Everybody in the crowd is looking at each other. Who is
brave enough to make the first move?

> At this, those who heard began to go away one at a time,
> the older ones first, until only Jesus was left, with the
> woman still standing there (John 8:9).

Everybody leaves. Nobody is without sin. No one is qualified
to start this woman's condemnation. Actually, there was
one person there who was qualified. There was one person
who had never sinned. There was one person who was
righteous enough to bring in God's condemnation. That
was Jesus. But Jesus didn't move.

This woman would have been absolutely terrified for her
life. A crowd had gathered to stone her to death. Imagine
what was going through her mind as one by one her
attackers sneaked away.

Jesus straightened up and asked her, 'Woman, where are
they? Has no one condemned you?'
'No one, sir,' she said (John 8:10–11a).

Jesus then says two extraordinary things to this woman.
Two things that summarise what it means to be set free by
Jesus' death and then live obediently in his freedom. The
two things Jesus says to this woman are meant for us as
well. They are truly liberating – and truly challenging.

Let's take them one by one:

Neither Do I Condemn You

Imagine the relief hearing this would have brought to this
woman. All her other accusers have left, but she is still there
with a holy rabbi. Will he condemn her?

'Then neither do I condemn you,' Jesus declared (John 8:11b).

If there's anyone in the world who has the right to condemn
someone for their sin, it is Jesus. He lived a perfect and
completely righteous life. No sin was ever found in him. He
is the only human who deserves absolutely no punishment
from God whatsoever. He is the ultimate judge, the Lord
of the universe and the highest power in all the cosmos.

If Jesus says, 'Neither do I condemn you,' – then you
are absolutely free, because there is no one else who *can*
condemn you.

Think of the sin that drags you down the most. Think of the times when you know you have failed God. Think of the moment when you let God down again. If you have truly come to Christ, then I want you to imagine Jesus looking you in the eye and saying, 'Neither do I condemn you.'

Freedom. No more fear. Only freedom.

Jesus has one more thing to say to this woman and one more thing to say to you.

Go And Leave Your Life Of Sin

> 'Then neither do I condemn you,' Jesus declared. 'Go now and leave your life of sin' (John 8:11).

What do you think this woman's reaction was when she heard Jesus say: 'Neither do I condemn you?'

What will she do now she is forgiven? Will she think, 'I've got away with it! As soon as Jesus leaves, I'll find another bloke and jump into bed with him?' No! Jesus did not save her life so that she could keep on sinning. Jesus set her free so that she could live in a brand-new way.

Jesus says exactly the same thing to you. Once he has forgiven you completely he then warns you to 'go and leave your life of sin'. If Jesus has set you free, then there is a whole new way of life that he wants you to live. A new life of freedom. A new life of obedience.

Jesus has been through the torture of the cross to pay for your sin so how could you ever go back to your old

153

ways of living? Jesus has set you free so then you are now free to obey. Jesus did not set you free so that you could keep on sinning. Jesus set you free so you could live in a brand-new way.

What sin are you hanging on to? Which piece of disobedience are you struggling to give up? Bring it now to Jesus – and hear him say these powerful words to you:

'Neither do I condemn you.'
'Now go and leave your life of sin.'

SECTION 6

The Last Bit

21

Free To Continue The Journey

We've been on an amazing journey together and we've discovered some mind-blowing things from God's Word.

God created you to be free. He designed you to depend on him. It's only when you remain dependent on God that you are truly free as a person. But we all prefer to do things our own way. We throw away our freedom and replace it with guilt. That guilt weighs us down now, and on the day that we meet again with our creator, that guilt will crush us.

Your day of freedom took place when Jesus was butchered on a cross. On that day, Jesus took all your guilt, all your sin, and all your punishment and dealt with it completely. He releases you to be free once again.

Now that Jesus has set you free, you are free to obey God and you are free to experience the joy of forgiving others.

God now has a whole life ahead of you that he wants you to enjoy as you live it for him.

If you are in Christ; if you are genuinely a Christian; then these promises from God hold true for you:

- God the Father created you to be free
- God the Son has died and risen to set you free
- God the Holy Spirit now dwells in you so you can live in God's freedom

So, how will you live the rest of your journey? Will you face it in your own strength or will you face it in the power of the God who has designed your future?

Only one of those ways will lead you to freedom.

Which way will you choose?

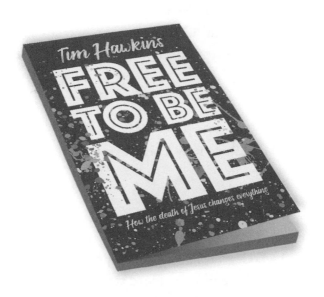

10Publishing is the publishing house of **10ofThose**.
It is committed to producing quality Christian
resources that are biblical and accessible.

www.10ofthose.com is our online retail arm selling
thousands of quality books at discounted prices.

For information contact: **info@10ofthose.com**
or check out our website: **www.10ofthose.com**